Just a Thought

A Time Alone with God

Just a Thought

By Rich LeBrun

All Rights Reserved. No part of this book may be reproduced in any form without permission in writing from the author except by a reviewer who wishes to quote brief passages in connection with a review written for inclusion in a magazine or newspaper. Proper credits required

Cover Design by Andrea Alva Viernes,

Virtually Done For You Digital Marketing

Copyright: © 2018 Rich LeBrun

Website: https://www.justathoughttoday.com/

All Rights reserved

ISBN-13: 978-1729693766

ISBN-10: 1729693768

Acknowledgement

We all know that we don't do life here on earth by ourselves for we are influenced daily by those we come in contact with, be it family, friends, pastors, colleagues or complete strangers. Each leave a mark on our lives that mold us into who we are today. I am grateful to each and every one of you. However, there are always those few that can have an impact in a way that can alter the direction of your life in a meaningful way and it is here I want to acknowledge you.

Although my journey toward God started way before I recognized Him working in my life, for me, the starting point happened in 1982. A man named Fred Iwen, who was my boss at the time, took me to lunch at his private club and shared stories about life and what it should mean to us as we walk this earth. He casually introduced the idea of biblical references where we could turn to see where life originated. From that day forward, I felt compelled to study the bible, so I could build a strong foundation to stand on.

It was years later that I gave my life to Christ and, unfortunately, I was never able to let Fred know the impact he made on me.

From that simple conversation to today the people who most influenced my faith are Bruce Graham, Don Jordan, Steve Kling, Dave Bye, Dean Loppnow, Dan Herzog, Ray Korizon, and my pastor, Bill Hybels. To all of you I am blessed to have you in my life.

To Cathy, my wife of 43 years, who has been my partner all the time that God was molding and shaping me. She saw the good, the bad and the ugly but was always there loving me. I can't find the words that can express my love for you.

And God... What can I say? You see me in a way that I never could have and have given me a purpose in life that I would never have dreamed of. I am eternally thankful.

Philippians 1:6 Being confident of this, that he who began a good work in you will carry it on to completion until the day of Christ Jesus.

Table of Contents

Introduction
Foreword

1. The Faster I Get There
2. Abundance
3. Coach Jesus
4. The Right Question
5. Sacrifice of Gratitude
6. Patient Hope
7. Give Us All Things
8. Measure of Faith
9. Was God Wrong?
10. A Personal Inventory
11. Everything New Under the Sun
12. I Don't Know
13. A Deeper Love
14. Pain
15. Too Much of God
16. Temptation All Around Us
17. What's so Special?
18. Remember Before You Pray
19. Very Tempting
20. Does It Work?
21. Freedom of Speech
22. Accept or Believe
23. I Am Mature in Christ
24. If You Are…
25. It's All Good
26. As a Man Believes
27. He Made Me This Way
28. Enduring Joy
29. Two Worlds

30 The Ask
31 Being Known
32 From God's Seat
33 The Right-Hand Man
34 Slavery is Still Alive
35 Nice Try, Satan
36 Break My Heart
37 Which is Harder?
38 It's Not All Bad
39 Don't Need to Come
40 True or False
41 This is the Day
42 I Can't Get No Satisfaction
43 A Little Work Plus a Little Faith
44 Forgiven
45 Take My Path
46 Threshold
47 Supreme Leadership
48 You Asked for It
49 Solomon's Second Chance
50 Getting Dressed
51 Going from Here to There
52 God's Job is Open, Applications Being Taken
53 Decision Time
54 Now What?
55 Approaching God
56 Finally Realized It
57 God's Promise
58 Surf's Up
59 Going Away Party
60 I Have a Plan for You
61 Is Love Enough?
62 It's No Surprise
63 Mind of Christ
64 Miracles
65 Moment by Moment
66 Prophet vs Savior

67 Run to Him
68 Temptation List
69 Work to Do
70 From Wailing to Dancing
71 Walking Through a Miracle
72 A Glimpse of Beauty in the Darkness
73 What is God Thinking?
74 God is Beautiful
75 The Magic Moment
76 Moving Forward
77 How to Stay Clear of God
78 In the Moment
79 When Do We Let God Off the Hook?
80 Fix Your Eyes Upon Jesus
81 What Can I Bring?
82 He had Everything, but He Possessed Nothing
83 Looking in All the Wrong Places
84 Peace
85 Do You Really Know Me?
86 Did God Really Say...?
87 Lean on Me
88 Trust
89 Patience
90 More Than a Memory
91 Love the Lord with All Your Soul
92 Storms
93 God's Economy
94 Define Faith
95 Be Careful What You Wish For
96 Great Expectations
97 Faith the Size of a Mustard Seed
98 What Do You See?
99 Can You See God?
100 The Battle Begins

Introduction

"The soul becomes dyed with the color of its thoughts."
Marcus Aurelius

Ever experienced that sudden rush of thoughts coming to your mind, especially in the morning?

Those thoughts that can make you realize the beauty of all the things surrounding you.

Thoughts that can comfort you that despite what's happening in our world, God is always there and always had been, all the time.

Thoughts that help us see the bright side on every dark side.

Thoughts that seem you are spending a time alone with God.

All of these positive thoughts by Rich LeBrun were put into this book to be shared with other people for us to find a peace whenever we are facing difficulties in life.

So, read on. Freshen up your minds and hearts and know that the great things in life are Just a Thought away.

Foreword

The following pages are a collection of thoughts over many years that arose from my time alone with God. Each one was based upon an impression or understanding that God revealed to me through reading scripture or books by Christian and non-Christian authors, as well as listening to sermons or worship music. Most are written between 3:00 am and 6:00 am. Why? I have no reason, yet this time in the day has become sacred to me. I look forward to it with great anticipation. It is during this time I feel the closest to God.

Over the years it is during this sacred time that I have wrestled with God through some of the darkest moments of my life. Fear, anxiety, doubt, sadness, anger, hatred, frustration and insecurity have all shown their ugly head and tried to convince me that God was not who he said he was. Yet each time I turned to God he proved faithful and was there to comfort me. There were major life and business decisions that came out of this time alone with him. There were tears and laughter and joy and ruthless trust moments as well.

One thing for certain, I know that each thought I had written down was from him. It would just come upon me as I was reading. Many times, I would read just a few words and I had to stop to write down what I was hearing. Other times I could go for days or weeks and read or engage in other ways and there would be nothing but silence on his part. But there was no doubt that when he had something to say I needed to capture it. I occasionally spend time reading over past notes and at times it's as if I am reading someone else's work for I don't remember writing them and yet, most of the time when I read them, I am encouraged and reminded of God's grace and goodness in my life.

I named these writings Just a Thought, for I never claimed that my writings were any more than my conversations between God and me. I am not a pastor nor educated in theology. My interpretation of scripture is solely based upon me being inspired by God to capture my/ his thoughts.

I do believe that God speaks to all who are willing to listen, and he can impart his wisdom as he wishes. I have come to enjoy writing these short snippets and hope that maybe by sharing these along the way in life with others that one may get a glimpse of the love of Christ. This would be my greatest joy.

There is no order to the book as this reflects the randomness of my time with God. I was tempted to organize them in various ways but then life just doesn't offer itself in organized patterns, so I thought I would leave them in the order that I was given them. I hope you enjoy a few of them as you make your way through the book. One thing I do know is that if you are indeed reading them, you have found the time to be alone with God and you too might hear his voice and reach for a pen and paper and write down a few words.

Just a Thought…

1
The Faster I Get There

The faster I turn back to Jesus, the faster my life gets back on track.

Prayer is the only way back to God yet, our pride, our distractions, our trust in worldly things will keep us away from turning to Him. However, we all will get to the point of realization that these things will never meet our needs and eventually, we fall on our knees and surrender and begin to pray.

The time in between our first thought that we need help, to the time we seek God, is referred to as the desert. The time we spend in the desert is totally up to us. We can either turn to God immediately, or we can wait. It's not that God is busy doing something else and we have to wait for Him. He is always there for us. I think this is where we take Him for granted. We know He is there, so we tell ourselves that we want to try handling this trial on our own. "God, we will call you when we need your help." How foolish we are. We soon will find that our trials will never leave us and had we turned to God earlier, many would have been resolved already.

The faster we turn to God, the faster our lives get back on track. Now, this doesn't mean the trials go away instantly, for trials can linger for days, weeks, months, and even years. But what does happen immediately upon turning to God in prayer is that we receive his strength to endure them, knowledge to understand, wisdom to discern, joy to persevere, and peace that can't be described.

How much time do you want to spend in the desert?

You are just a prayer away of turning back home.

Think about it, but don't take too long.

Just a Thought…

2
Abundance

God has pointed out that He has an abundance of everything we need; resources, forgiveness, mercy, grace, power, love, peace, patience, kindness, goodness, joy, and restraint, enough so that there is an unending supply. He is searching for people who will be willing to share these things with other people, so He can further His kingdom here on earth.

The problem is that we are hoarders! The simplest form in which we see this is with our money. We may even tithe but even that is a mind game. We hesitantly write those checks, so we must learn to open up our grip on money. This comes from a fear that we will run out and don't trust God that He will replenish our resources. However, He says He will but not on a one for one basis, but in a multiplying effect.

What we don't recognize so easily is our hoarding of things like our time, our love, our patience, our grace, our mercy, for we subconsciously feel we will run out of these as well.

Have you ever said, I just don't have any more to give? I have no more time to share or love to give out or I'm out of patience? This may be true when we rely on ourselves to be the producer and supplier of these resources. Yet, when we turn to God as our true resource, He who has an abundance of all we need and who will gladly restore our supply. This pleases God as He can see His resources being put to work. When He says He will fill our cup till it overflows, He means it! He is giddy with anticipation when He gets the opportunity to share more of what He has. What parent doesn't want to bless their children?

So be generous, give as much away of yourself as you can. You will find freedom and joy in doing so. Pay no attention to Satan's whisper telling you that you better hang on to that forgiveness, that love, that dollar for it might be your last. Give freely. For giving is living.

Just a Thought…

Coach Jesus

I find it interesting that we will pay for personal trainers to teach us and talk us through exercise routines and allow them to bring our bodies to stressful and painful places, for we know afterwards we will receive the benefit. We pay for career coaches to encourage us, guide us, tell us the hard truths and challenge us in order that we may find a more profitable and meaningful career. We pay for therapists who will listen to our woes, allow for us to be vulnerable and then gently guide us back to a place we can now cope. We pay for financial planners, tax advisors, weight loss counselors, and on and on it goes.

Yet, we have a Lord that can guide us with the power of almighty God, who is with us each moment of every day ready to teach us and guide us in our relationships, finances, careers, our bodies, our minds, our parenting, and more, however, we chose to pay outsiders for this service?

God is not telling us not to use the help from others. In fact, He encourages us to share our lives that way yet, He does tell us to seek him first, His guidance, His advice, His comfort, His strength. To submit to His plan and purpose and from there He will bring people in our lives to join us in our journey here on earth.

For some reason, we find it easier to write a check or take a pill before we seek out the Lord. Access to God was paid for by Jesus' death on the cross so we who believe now have a lifetime free pass to come to Him. Put your checkbook away, come to Jesus freely and let Him be your coach whispering in your ear all day words of encouragement, wisdom, comfort, and feel His strength as you grab hold of His hand and begin the climb of the mountain that is challenging you. At the end of the day, rejoice with Him in your victory and sleep in peace as He watches over you planning for the day ahead.

Just a Thought...

4

The Right Question

Why doesn't God do everything we ask?

When I read this question, I paused long enough to ask another question, that is, what right do I have to expect God to do anything I ask? For those who don't know God, He is not someone to turn to put forth these requests for they don't acknowledge His existence. Yet, as soon as we discover that God is truly real, we somehow think we found a genie of sorts where we can go and have all our dreams come true.

How wrong we are in this thinking.

For if we came to know the living God, we would know His character, His heart, His plan. Nowhere does it say that He will grant us anything that is apart from His will. Yet, it says throughout the Bible that He does indeed give us the desires of our hearts when they are aligned with His will. His will is for us to love Him and His people. Simple as that. In order to love Him, we need to stay close to Him, learn about Him, seek Him, glorify Him, spend time with Him. The closer we come to Him the more we see His heart in all things. We see that He desires to love us and provide for us and protect us. He desires that we have life in all its fullness and that we receive a joy and peace that transcends all understanding.

He also knows that we need a savior in order to operate in this world and fend off Satan's attack. Because He designed us, He knows what brings us the most joy before we do. So, in a sense, we don't need to ask Him for anything for He has already given it to us. It's there for the taking if we look for it. Oh, it's not a car or house or job or money or health or companion. No, it's better than that. It's the freedom to not need any of those things. Now the fun part, should we be so close to Him, He may indeed give us these as well if He found that they could and would be used for his glory.

There is a strange sense of freedom when we lay down the need to ask God for anything except to know Him more. Our attitude changes from expecting anything to receiving everything. Our eyes and hearts are opened to take in all that God already has given and promised us, leaving nothing we could ever dream of asking that could be greater.

If this is true then, when we ask for anything other than to be close to God, then we are inserting that thing in front or in place of God. Do we really think the God of the universe does not know we might need a car or a job or food or clothing or a friend or comfort or healing? Is He asleep in heaven or busy in meetings or traveling and wasn't aware of our needs? God is with us 24/7. He never leaves us. This means He is never not in tune to what we need. Never. For anyone of us who have walked with God for any length of time all know this to be true, that the road always leads back to God. We may start out seeking some worldly answer to our questions or needs but in the end, it's always God that we come to when the world comes up short.

The time between when we start and when we submit to God can be shortened by our own free will. The quicker we come to Jesus, the quicker we get our answer.

The question is no longer "Why doesn't God do everything we ask?", but rather, "How can we find ways to thank God for all that He has given us?"

Just a Thought…

5
Sacrifice of Gratitude

There was a time in biblical history that sacrifice was an actual ritual intended to honor God. Yet, over time, it became a task rather than out of love and God saw our hearts become hardened. Today we are still called to sacrifice, to let go of our selfish ways and be thankful for how God has blessed us for Him to continue to mold us in His image.

In contemplating this, I find it odd that we call it sacrifice to merely be grateful for the gift of Christ's death for us to give us eternal life. A simple thank you throughout the day, a giving spirit, a generous heart. Really, these are sacrifices? So, someone gives me a gift and I say thank you and I'm sacrificing something? I don't get it, but then I know it's true.

We find this every day with children who take for granted the food on the table, clothes on their back, shelter that protects them. You never hear of them being grateful for these things; it becomes expected and ultimately demanded and criticized. We are all children of God and have the same spirit about us. God provides for our mere existence, breath in our lungs, sunshine, warmth, a planet to live on, resources to mine, companionship, and yes, food, clothing, shelter. We too, take this for granted and have come to expect it and judge it every day according to our liking.

Would it be or is it really that hard to say thank you? I guess in order to be grateful, I must acknowledge that these were and are gifts, and that I have nothing to do with them. If I'm truthful, I admit that they can be taken away. The sacrifice is tied to the inner battle of self. If I break it down to the most minute segment of time, to say thank you is a fraction of a second. So, it's not the words or the time it takes to say them, it's a matter of the heart leading up to the verbal appreciation. That is where the battle lies.

We don't see it because we are so busy that it's ignored or at best, added to a to-do list. Without the right heart, it's no different than bringing live animals to the altar for sacrifice out of a resentful heart. God turns His back on these.

In today's busy world, we must get quiet long enough to remember the things we are to be thankful for.

When doing this, we go from a hard heart to a joyful and grateful one. We then desire to say thanks to our God for we connect with His love for us. We become humbled by the wonder and amazement of God's blessings in our life. We go from expecting to fear of losing them.

Just a Thought…

6
Patient Hope

Romans 8:21-22
"That the creation itself will be set free from its bondage to corruption and obtain the freedom of the glory of the children of God. For we know that the whole creation has been groaning together in the pains of childbirth until now."

Creation's corruption and groaning,
Terrorism wreaking havoc
Politics expressing hatred
Sex scandals and abuse rampant
Financial greed causing distrust
Pornography in every home
Random killings even in sacred places
Nuclear threats overhead
The U.S. in debt over its head
Sex trafficking a number one crime
Divorce at 50%
Gay and transgender movement front and center
Faith in God losing ground
Prayer removed from school
Fear and anxiety at an all-time high
Racial tension brewing
Natural disasters sweeping across the country
Addictions taking no prisoners
Technology stealing the minds of our children intentionally

I now see the groaning of creation trying to shake off the filth of the dirt these things bring.

Oh, for the day that the Lord returns to restore His world.
We cry out, return father, yet He still seeks those who are lost.

As much as we see the ugliness of the world all around us, if we stay still long enough, we will see that there is another world in the midst of all this darkness. We can see God at work, transforming lives. We can see the best of humanity come out in the worst of tragedies. We see bold statements of generosity overshadowing greed, we see peace that transcends our understanding in those who follow Christ. We notice the sun still rises, beautiful sunsets still paint the sky, stars still guide us, blue still backdrops beautiful clouds, birds fly freely, wind blows at will and trees still stretch their limbs toward heaven. With all the death that surrounds us a simple birth of a child restores our joy. Love still works as the ultimate medicine for the heart, a smile can still break the most stubborn, and a helping hand always soothes the soul.

Yes, we wait and cry out for Jesus to quickly return and yet we wait in patience through hope.

Romans 8:25
But if we hope for what we do not see, we wait for it with patience.

Just a Thought…

7
Give Us All Things

Romans 8:31-32
God's Everlasting Love
"What then shall we say to these things? If God is for us, who can be against us? He who did not spare his own Son but gave him up for us all, how will He not also with Him graciously give us all things?"

Give us all things? We love this verse and especially the very last four words.

Give us all things.
What things will he give us? A house, a car, a spouse, a job, healing, money, good grades, a trip, food, clothing, shelter, a friend, peace patience, love, joy, what indeed will He give us? God tells us that He will work out things for the good of those who love Him and are called according to His purpose.

Romans 8:28
"And we know that for those who love God all things work together for good, for those who are called according to his purpose."

God also says the fruits of the spirit are love, joy, peace, patience, kindness, goodness, and self-control. Are these the things He will give us for they align with His purpose?

God describes other gifts He gives when He says not to worry about food, clothing, or shelter but to seek Him first then we will receive those things as well.

Matthew 6:33
"But seek first the kingdom of God and his righteousness, and all these things will be added to you."

Is there a line in the sand or a list of sorts that God uses to determine what things he will give us? He goes on to offer us the desires of our hearts when we delight ourselves in Him. What are our desires of the heart and do they automatically change when we filter them through our delight in Christ? Even more profound, God tells us He knows what we need before we do.

Matthew 6:8
"Do not be like them, for your Father knows what you need before you ask him."

This becomes an obvious theme. God indeed will give us all things. Might they be materialistic, relational, financial, occupational? Sure, however, they will all be tied to His purpose and filtered through our love for him. When our hearts are focused on Him the things of the world lose their luster and become strangely dim. We will find that when we seek Him with all our strength, hearts, and minds that all we want to do is to please Him. God sees this and then knows what worldly things we need to provide and protect us and to bring us joy.

For some, it may be more money for God sees how generosity is one's gift. For another, it may be a big house, for hospitality is how they serve God. It might be a high position of influence for God gifted that person with exceptional leadership skills that can influence people towards Christ. The secret is when we are aligned with God, the things we receive will have a different meaning. We will see clearly that they are God's provision and are to be used for his Glory.

So yes – if God sacrificed his Son for us, indeed he will give us all things in order that we can further His Son's purpose here on earth. To Glorify the Father.

Imagine God looking at two options contemplating which gift to give a person, one being a sale that will generate a large commission which the money will be used to satisfy a selfish desire, or a challenge that will draw the person closer to Himself. Which would He choose? Both are gifts. What would you do?

Just a Thought…

8
Measure of Faith

Romans 12:3 Gifts of Grace
"For by the grace given to me I say to everyone among you not to think of himself more highly than he ought to think, but to think with sober judgment, each according to the measure of faith that God has assigned."

This verse mentions that God has assigned different levels of faith to people.

My first question is why? My second question is, does this mean God likes one person more than another? Why wouldn't God give His children the same amount of faith? But then again, why doesn't God give each person the same amount of ability? In a world of comparison, this feeds right into jealousy, resentment, and performance. Was that God's intent?

From the very beginning, by God creating a man and a woman, we see that He created unique individuals with different bodies, abilities, and purposes. Therefore, Paul found it necessary to put this verse down in writing. We are to have sober thoughts of who we are individually and when we look at one another. Sober, meaning clear thoughts, without judgment, jealousy or resentment. As humans, we have this need to feel either superior or inferior towards others. It's very difficult to look at another person and not subconsciously size them up.

We then find ourselves associating a level of favor as to why one person appears to have more or less of ability, attractiveness, wisdom, power, position etc. We can't accept who we are as God made us. God doesn't see it that way. For He loves each person the exact same. He sees no differences when it comes to His love for us. If He did, then Jesus' death would have had qualifiers attached to it, such as He died for the poor and not the rich, the weak and not the strong, the powerful and not the servants. He knew that we would have this tendency so His way of leveling the playing field is saying, God so loved the world and that means everyone. The qualifier He did use was belief. Yet, by using belief as the differentiator, He understood that no matter how we looked, the position we held, the wealth we accumulated, or physical or mental abilities we have, we all have the same ability to believe.

Faith is faith, so why different measures? It makes sense that God would allocate various measures of faith that would match up to our various abilities. Yet, note that large amounts of faith can be seen in the meekest, the humble, and the impoverished. The story of the woman with two mites comes to mind.

We also see where God says to those in high position – oh you of little faith!

Faith is a matter of the heart. Furthermore, a measure means that our faith can increase as well as we learn more to trust God. It is fluid. It would make no sense to give an infant a whole steak to eat the same as an adult. Yet, both have the same capability to eat, yet each have a different ability to digest it.

God knows the right amount of faith we each need, yet, He has no limitations on how much we can have. God loves seeing our faith grow and is ready to pour out more along the way. May we not compare but rather encourage one another to develop our faith in God.

Just a Thought…

9
Was God Wrong?

Job 40:8
"Will you even put me in the wrong?
Will you condemn me that you may be in the right?"

Lord, every time I question my life and doubt You, I make You wrong by saying I know better how things should be. I can't serve two masters, it's either you or my flesh. Either You are God or You're not.

If You are God, then everything about You is true. Everything, Your power, Your grace, Your love, Your creation, Your truth, Your way, Your forgiveness, Your salvation. Everything. This means Your tactics or strategy are for me to come to know You better; Your purpose for doing so and Your need to use trials as Your tool that I may experience a deeper love for You.

My goal is not perfection. God, You will transform me into your likeness. I can't do this. My goal is to love You more in the process.

There is no one righteous, not one. None ever reached the goal of perfection this side of heaven. The greatest spiritual people known on earth claim their wretchedness. But to say Your will not mine with a pure heart, is the best we can love God. Cancel the lie once and for all that you must perform at a certain level to please God.

Adam, Noah, Moses, Joshua, Jacob, Abraham, Paul, David, Mathew, Mark, Luke, John, Brother Lawrence, Mother Theresa, Billy Graham, Oswald Chambers, everyone falls short. Knowing this allows you to freely love them and yourself. No more pressure. Each one learned that the faster they turned to Jesus, the faster they were to receive his peace.

Just a Thought…

10
A Personal Inventory

Personal inventory:

It's that time of year to stop everything a take a personal inventory and spiritual check-up one would say. Remember that this is a journey.

Here a few questions you might ponder along the way:

1. Do I know Jesus Christ as my personal savior?

2. Am I spending time with God each day through prayer, reading the Bible, or serving others?

3. Am I more loving, forgiving, and accepting of others and myself?

4. Have I become more generous with my money, possessions, talents, and my time?

5. Have I confessed my sins that I'm aware of to God?

6. Am I more at peace with God?

7. Do my friends, children, family, and spouse or loved one, know they are loved by me?

8. Am I growing closer to God or farther away from Him?

Wherever you see yourself needing to grow, seek God to help you.

Just a Thought…

11
Everything New Under the Sun

Every day is a new day.

Are there times when you think today is just the same as yesterday and tomorrow will be the same as today? Do you ever think that nothing ever changes, that maybe the rut of routine is dragging you down?

Maybe even stolen your joy for the day?

You might be saying to yourself,
Same old boring job
Same old house that needs repair
Same addiction that I can't beat
Same old argument that I have with my spouse
Same depressed feelings that I can't seem to shake
Same town I live in
Same
Same…

Nothing is going to change, I'm bored, I'm depressed, I don't care anymore, everything just looks grey to me.

At times, life just appears to be blah, boring, just plain, not exciting anymore. Yet, if we would turn right instead of left down that same street we have traveled for the last ten years, or drive to a town we never saw before, or try a different food, say hi to a new person, watch a different movie, put our clothes on in a different order, change the radio station, go out of the house at different times of the day, we would find that every day, every moment of every day, is new and exciting. The world is ever changing right in front of us!

New songs are sung, pictures painted, babies born, flowers planted, people relocating, homes built, technology invented, books written, mysteries being unveiled. It has been said there is nothing new under the sun. I say there is something new under the sun every second of the day.

We are new every second just by breathing and walking this earth. Every step we take can be different if we look at change in the simplest term. A new idea crosses your mind, a taste of food, a simple paint stroke, a note changes in a melody, a physical experience, an emotional response, a sound, a breeze across your face, everything is new. In fact, it is impossible for things to stay the same. Our mere existence as humans and creations profound reality will not allow it.

Try it and see. Stand still, without a thought, without an action, and see what changes around you.

Life can be full of anticipation if we look for changes rather than trying to contain it. The attempt to contain only creates stress; embracing it brings excitement.

Psalm 5:3
"Morning by morning I lay my request before you and wait expectantly."

Lamentations 3:22-23
"The steadfast love of the Lord never ceases;
his mercies never come to an end;
they are new every morning;
great is your faithfulness."

The next step you take, the next word out of your mouth, the next thought, breath, touch, sound, emotion, or prayer can be and is something new.

Embrace it.

SIT QUIETLY WITH ME, letting all your fears and worries bubble up to the surface of your consciousness. There, in the Light of My Presence, the bubbles pop and disappear.

Jesus Calling: Don't hold fear and worry down. Let it ride in the light of Christ. Pray, talk with someone, write it, sing it, paint it. Just don't contain it.

Lord, as I write this, I too, sit at a crossroad. Will I choose joy and anticipation about my next move or fear and worry? The move is coming regardless.

I see my job, my spouse, my possessions, relationships, faith, all in a new light.

This day is for trouble and excitement. The good news, God has taken care of the trouble and at the same time, delivers something new to enjoy.

I say everything is new under the sun!!!

Just a Thought…

12
I Don't Know

I sincerely don't know.

I literally don't know what is going to happen one minute from now. I concede that the less amount of time between now and the very next minute, makes it easier to say I know something.

However I don't. I don't know where the wind will blow, that my body won't experience something good or bad, I don't know the next phone call or email that could alter my course, or where the next song, book, sermon, that will guide me. The very best I can do is to eat right, exercise, pray, read, meditate, plan, in order to have an influence of the next moment. If I did every one of those things in the most perfect and Godly way, my chances will increase that my next moment could be fruitful.

But truth be told, all I'm doing is hedging my bets. Don't believe me, just read the paper.

Killings at concerts or church services
Betrayal by a friend or spouse
The doctor visit that informs the athlete he has cancer
The pastor who falls to pornography
The 40-year employee who gets laid off
The car that crashes into you unexpectantly

God reminds us that while we don't know at the same time He does, we are called to live in the moment and in return He will reward us with his peace. We can say we don't know with a sense of confidence, giving up the need or right to know to Jesus the one who only truly does.

Just a Thought…

13
A Deeper Love

Regarding your time with God, don't look for the pleasure payoff. It's best to pursue this relationship because we love Him and because it's God's will for us.

It just dawned on me that there is a deeper love that I can have for God than I thought.

I currently love being with God for all the fruits of the spirit that He provides.
I love receiving His peace, patience, kindness, and joy.
I love receiving His comfort and courage, and of course, there is the gift of eternity.
Yet, as I pause for a minute, I see I'm a consumer of God's goodness.
I love Him for what I can receive from Him.

I see now that there is a deeper love that I desire to pursue.
I want to love God because of who He is and what He already has done, by giving His Son to die for us. Can that be enough? Should we receive nothing else? Can this be enough reason to love God? The irony is that even if we can get to this level of love, God has a way of seeing that we receive the other gifts as well.

He just desires our hearts to be in the right place. We can see this with Shadrach, Meshach, and Abednego when they were before the king.

Daniel 3:17-18
"If this be so, our God whom we serve is able to deliver us from the burning fiery furnace, and He will deliver us out of your hand, O king. ***But if not****, be it known to you, O king, that we will not serve your gods or worship the golden image that you have set up."*

Will we love God even if we receive nothing in return?

There is a long list of those who did not receive all they hoped for yet continued to love God.

Read Hebrews 11.

I think of Mother Theresa who, for most of her life, felt God abandoned her yet, saw a deeper love for Him regardless.

Lord, I desire this depth of love with my mouth. Help me to reach it with my heart.

Can I do this with a joyful spirit and not with a scowl as that of a martyr?

I love you, Lord.

Just a Thought…

14
Pain

There is no formula to avoid pain, suffering, or distress, as it is in the world all around us. Yet even Jesus experienced the same.

The only solution is Jesus, not anything I can do.

The pain may never leave, or, at best, we will get a season without it, but be assured it will return.

Jesus will give us strength and comfort in the form of peace and even joy in the midst. He never promised to eliminate pain this side of heaven. He did promise to be with us in it.

The biggest lie is that we think we can do something about it apart from Jesus.

Just a Thought…

15
Too Much of God

Can we ever have too much of God?

There is a saying that always haunted me. It is "You can have as much of God as you want".

We say we want all of God. What would that look like? Do you conjure up a picture of floating on a cloud, always smiling and happy, no worries, no trials, no temptations, no struggles, filled with joy, always making the right decisions, and doing the right things? Would you see yourself as humble, a good servant, steward, and generous?

Will we ever get all of God we want this side of heaven? I propose it's unlikely as it's not a destination we reach, rather a journey we experience. We certainly start out wanting to have all of God and then because of the evil that surrounds us and the selfishness of our nature, we find ourselves turning away from God even if we desire not to. God knows this about us and that is why the Apostle Paul says in Philippians 1:6:

"And I am sure of this, that he who began a good work in you will bring it to completion at the day of Jesus Christ."

Brother Lawrence wrote a book called "Practicing the Presence of God".

What I feel Brother Lawrence was conveying is that, experiencing the presence of God is indeed something that can increase greatly in our daily life and part of that is to reduce the amount of doubt, guilt, or condemnation we feel when we come up short along the way.

Brother Lawrence would quickly admit his sin and then immediately continue with his praise of God. He did not dwell on his sin. He accepted that it was part of his life and though he did not like it, he knew that God did not count it against him as long as his heart was in the right place.

So sincerely wanting all of God is a matter of the heart. The first step is to know that He loves to hear this. The next step is to know that He has made all of himself available. The third step is to let Him work this out in you and understand you can't do it yourself.

Your job is to keep your heart in the right place. Brother Lawrence said he does this by having a lofty view of who God is and a lofty love for him, the rest God takes care of.

Each moment of your day God is giving you a piece of Him for you to practice with. As you experience Him, you find that you see how you have grown in having more of Him. This will show up in both internal and external ways. You will think new thoughts, desire to serve or to give, find new ways to forgive or accept others and yourself. You will increase in strength when trials come your way and experience new levels of peace, appreciate more of creation, and your mind will return to God quicker.

I don't think Brother Lawrence hit his goal this side of heaven, but I do feel he learned to enjoy the journey in a much greater way.

Just a Thought…

16
Temptation All Around Us

He said to the woman, "Did God actually say You shall not eat of any tree in the garden?" –
Genesis 3:1

Doubt was the weapon Satan used with Eve. It's the same weapon he uses today. The key thing to know is, it isn't the weapon as much as there was Satan lurking around to use it. It's important to notice that Satan approached Eve. Until that time, Eve was content just enjoying her day never expecting that she was going to be approached and challenged in a way that would change history forever.

One could argue why God planted the tree in the first place. Yet if not for a tree, Satan would have found another object or emotion to entice Eve to doubt God, for humans are emotional beings with a free will planted within us.

We need to know that sin and temptation are all around us every day. It will find us – we don't have to look for it. Satan is alive and well trying to take us away from God. Instead of apples, he will bring opportunity, beautiful people, money, position, prosperity, new technology, more kinds of freedom: freedom of speech, freedom of expression, more thrills, and with all, he will ask us did God actually say…

Do not judge?
Humble yourself?
Give to the poor?
Do not lust?
Care for the widow?
Love your spouse?
Train up your kids to love God?
To go the extra mile?
Not to worry?
Not to be anxious?
Flee from sin?
To trust Him?

To tithe?
Train up our minds?
Do not let anything have mastery over me?
My body is a temple?
Don't argue?
Build up others?
Do not consider myself better than others?
That He has a plan for me?
I can do all things through Christ?
That He has overcome the world?
To believe in Jesus and I will have eternal life?
That Jesus is the only way back to God?
The wages of sin is death?
That all have fallen short of the glory of God?
To be still and know He is God?
Don't be anxious about anything?
To love the church?
To confess my sins?

The moment we awake sin is all around us, but if we look heavenwards, we can see through the darkness that surrounds us and see creation, people, and life as God intended.

God is not far away. He is beside us and before us. He will guide us through this day. Our faith is in Him and His ability, not ours.

We don't hold His hand with trepidation or hide behind Him, but rather walk hand and hand with boldness, joy, peace, untouchable by Satan.

Be strong and courageous today!

Just a Thought…

17
What's so Special?

Jesus says to live fully in the present, depending on Him each moment. What's so special about a moment? As I begin to slow down my mind to capture a single moment, I must admit I have asked myself this very question. There is even a sense of boredom as I tell myself that staying in the moment takes away all my anticipation, planning, vision, and eagerness.

My mind had been racing with thoughts about what I'm going to be doing later today, tomorrow, and in the distant future. When these thoughts are good, creative, and hopeful, I want to be there rather than in the current moment. Think about when you were planning a vacation, starting a new job in a few days, designing your wedding day, or awaiting your child to be born. Those future days are filled with excitement.

However, we all have experienced just the opposite. Days ahead that are going to be filled with grief, suffering, sorrow. A pending divorce, an ongoing physical pain that gets worse by the day, a job layoff, or financial ruin. There is nothing more we desire than for those days to never come.

Yet, in both future good or bad situations, if we were to train our mind to slow down to the very nanosecond of the current moment, we will see something that transcends the future and overshadows the past. We will be conscious of the very breath we breathe, the minute intricacies of every part of our body, the smell in the air, that tingly feeling of a touch, the colors around us, the chirping of the birds, the arms of God wrapped around us, a peace that can't be described, and humility that brings a smile, a confidence in a powerful God, strength and courage that exceeds our own physical abilities, love at its deepest level, wisdom that only Solomon could boast of, and the fruits of the spirit, hope, patience, and joy. We can experience each one of these things in every moment, at any time, in any place. There are no restrictions or rules. No price, position, or performance that is required. It's available to all people everywhere.

The scripture says, 'Be still and know that He is God.'

A moment. What's so special? The answer is everything.

Take a moment and experience it for yourself.

Just a Thought…

18
Remember Before You Pray

"Remember what God has already done for you. If God never did anything else for you, he would still deserve your continual praise for the rest of your life because of what Jesus did for you on the cross." – Rick Warren, The Purpose Driven Life

Oh Lord, how I forget so easily the sacrifice You paid that I might be with You in eternity.

I sit here daily pouring out my prayers to You asking for things, for help, for wisdom, for safety, for comfort, for healing, each time forgetting what You have already done for me. Each time I submit my request without first remembering your suffering that I shall be free, negates Your gift, Your perseverance, Your love, Your hope, Your joy, Your peace, Your confidence, Your comfort, Your heart, Your desire that I might trust you enough with my life as You trusted me with Yours. Lord, You are betting on the fact that by sacrificing Jesus by this ultimate act of love, I or we will finally come to You, having the same desire to be with You forever as you do for us.

Lord, may each time before I pray remember Jesus on the cross.

Unfortunately, I forget the cruel details of the agonizing sacrifice God made on my behalf. Familiarity breeds complacency. Even before His crucifixion, the Son of God was stripped naked, beaten until almost unrecognizable, whipped, scorned and mocked, crowned with thorns, and spit on contemptuously. Abused and ridiculed by heartless men, He was treated worse than an animal. Then, nearly unconscious from blood loss, He was forced to drag a cumbersome cross up a hill, was nailed to it, and was left to die the slow, excruciating torture of death by crucifixion. While His lifeblood drained out, hecklers stood by and shouted insults, making fun of His pain and challenging His claim to be God. Next, as Jesus took all of mankind's sin and guilt on Himself, God looked away from that ugly sight, and Jesus cried out in total desperation, "My God, my God, why have you forsaken me?"

Jesus could have saved Himself but then, He could not have saved you!

It wasn't a surprise to You Lord what was going to happen to You on that day. You knew it as evidenced by Your plea in the garden that this might be taken from You. But knowing there was no other way possible that You could save us from our sins in order that we could be reunited with You forever. You took a deep breath, looked beyond what You were going to have to go through and focused on the goal, took that first step and began walking towards Your brutal death.

For the joy set before You, You endured the cross.

How deeply engrained in You that picture must have been of us being together for eternity, that joy would be the emotion that carried You through until the end. You could see Your resurrection, You could see our faces as You appeared before the disciples. Yet Lord this day, You wish that I not forget that day. That I remind myself the degree that You went to let me know You love me and to not worry today, but to love You and Your people and that everything else will be and was already taken care of.

Lord, I love You so much.

Light of the world you stepped down into darkness
Opened my eyes, let me see
Beauty that made this heart adore You
Hope of a life spent with You

Here I am to worship, here I am to bow down
Here I am to say that you're my God
You're altogether lovely, altogether worthy
Altogether wonderful to me

King of all days oh so highly exalted
Glorious in heaven above
Humbly You came to the earth You created
All for love's sake became poor

Here I am to worship, here I am to bow down
Here I am to say that you're my God
You're altogether lovely, altogether worthy
Altogether wonderful to me

Well, I'll never know how much it cost
To see my sin upon that cross
Well, I'll never know how much it cost
To see my sin upon that cross

Song written by: Tim Hughes

Just a Thought…

19
Very Tempting

Matthew 4:1-11
The Temptation of Jesus
"Then Jesus was led up by the Spirit into the wilderness to be tempted by the devil. And after fasting forty days and forty nights, he was hungry. And the tempter came and said to him, "If you are the Son of God, command these stones to become loaves of bread." But he answered, "It is written, "Man shall not live by bread alone but by every word that comes from the mouth of God." Then the devil took him to the holy city and set him on the pinnacle of the temple and said to him, "If you are the Son of God, throw yourself down, for it is written, "He will command his angels concerning you," and "On their hands they will bear you up, lest you strike your foot against a stone."
Jesus said to him, "Again it is written. You shall not put the Lord your God to the test." Again, the devil took him to a very high mountain and showed him all the kingdoms of the world and their glory. And he said to him, "All these I will give you, if you will fall down and worship me." Then Jesus said to him, "Be gone, Satan! For it is written, "You shall worship the Lord your God and him only shall you serve." Then the devil left him, and behold, angels came and were ministering to him.

Satan uses things such as power, greed, prestige, possessions, ego, money, and lust to tempt us. These are his tools. They are easily identified when you contrast them with God's fruits of the spirit, which are love, patience, kindness, peace, joy, goodness, and self-control.

So, if God were to tempt us, it might look something like this:

Matthew 4:1-11 The Temptation of Rich
"Then Rich was led up by the Spirit into the wilderness to be tempted by Jesus. And after fasting forty days and forty nights, he was hungry. And Jesus came and said to him, "If you are God's child, take these loaves of bread and give them to those who are hungry. But Rich said, I won't for I fear I will have nothing to eat for me and my family. Then Jesus took him to the holy city and set him on the pinnacle of the temple and said to him, "If you are a child of God, surrender all you have to the holy God,

for it is written, "He will command his angels concerning you," and "On their hands they will bear you up."

Again, Rich said, "I can't for it took me my entire career to get to where I am. What will everyone think of me?" Again, Jesus took him to a very high mountain and showed him all the kingdoms of the world and their glory. And he said to him, "All these I will give you, if you will fall down and worship me." Then Rich said to him, "Be gone, Jesus! For it is written, I fear that if I worship you that you will ask that I give all that I have away to the poor or the widow and I will be left with nothing." Then Jesus left him, and behold, Satan's angels came and were ministering to him."

Jesus will encourage, prompt, convict, nudge, challenge, and stretch us to die to ourselves each day through acts of surrender, generosity, serving, caring, and loving those around us and by releasing our grip on the things we have acquired so they may be used for His glory.

God's temptations will always be to the glory of Himself, the care of another, and the spiritual growth of each one who believes in Him.

Just a Thought…

20
Does It Work?

Does it work? This is how the purist's test whether Jesus and Christianity are true. What do WE do when we want to prove something is true or not? We test it, don't we?

Like that car? Take a test drive.
Wonder if you're pregnant? Take a pregnancy test.
Do you understand a subject? Take a test.
Will this product sell? Do a test market study.
Is the water cold? Put your toe in and test it.
Do I like this food? Take a taste test.

Is it really that simple but yet profound that we could consider our entire faith, and, for that matter, eternity could be based on a simple testing of the truth? What would the test even look like? Let's test the following and see what happens; be sincere in doing the following:

Love somebody today
Serve someone today
Give some money away to a poor person
Read the Bible
Pray to Jesus
Attend a church service
Forgive your worst enemy
Encourage someone
Listen to Christian music
Read a Christian book
Feed a homeless person
Care for a widow
Sit on a mountaintop and take in creation

If Jesus and what He taught is true, it will become evident in you. A literal transformation will begin to take place.

God says, "Seek me and you will find me." Let's test him at His word. What do you have to lose? Better yet, what do you have to gain?

Just a Thought…

21
Freedom of Speech

Psalms 139:4
⁴ Before a word is on my tongue you, Lord, know it completely.

Why does the Lord know what we speak before we say it? It's because He knows the condition of our hearts. He knows that if it is filled with love, words of kindness, encouragement, empathy will be voiced. Yet if the heart is angry, resentful, prideful, words of like kind will also come out.

Luke 6:45
⁴⁵The good person out of the good treasure of his heart produces good and the evil person out of his evil treasure produces evil, for out of the abundance of the heart his mouth speaks.

God is always concerned about our heart and is trying to transform it to express love but knows first that we must trust Him with it.

If the saying goes, hurting people hurt people so then, loving people love people. This is the goal of God's work in us and through us.

Take a moment and assess your heart and see what condition it is in. If it is hurting, then be cautious how you speak to others. On the other hand, if it is at peace and filled with love, then, go about your day sharing freely the love you are experiencing.

Just a Thought…

22
Accept or Believe

"Everything is made to center upon the initial act of "accepting" Christ (a term, incidentally, which is not found in the Bible), and we are not expected thereafter to crave any further revelation of God to our spirit."
– The Pursuit of God, AW Tozer

Who would have thought that such a fine line could make all the difference? It's so subtle it's hardly noticed. Can you see it? The difference between – I accept Jesus as my savior vs. I believe in Jesus as my savior.

Why is this so hard to detect? When you finally see it, you then know why it makes all the difference in the world for our faith. Let's take a closer look.

John 3:16
For God So Loved the World
16 For God so loved the world that he gave his one and only Son, that whoever believes in him shall not perish but have eternal life.

There it is. Whoever believes!

Could you accept a gift and still not believe? Imagine if your enemy handed you a gift for their gratitude towards something, could you see yourself being suspicious as to their real motive even though you accepted the gift? Sure, we do this all the time passing judgment as to why the giver is being so generous. We say things like "I wonder what they are after?"

Now consider using the word "believe". This word is finite. It's an act of commitment.

You will believe thereby concluding something is real or not. You cross over, give of yourself thereby, being vulnerable. Belief had to be final. A small but powerful word.

By comparison, using the word accept you still have the option to believe or not. To believe means there is no turning back. There's only the deciding to no longer believe, which again is final in its nature.

When you believe Christ died for you, it should trigger a pursuit of God which says "Okay God, now what? Show me more what it means to believe in Jesus." The struggle will be to continue the believing.

Mark 9:24
[24] Immediately the boy's father exclaimed, "I do believe; help me overcome my unbelief!"

Satan is more concerned with those who believe that his goal is to cause you to doubt your decision.

And the woman said to the serpent, "We may eat of the fruit of the trees in the garden, but God said, you shall not eat of the fruit of the tree that is in the midst of the garden, neither shall you touch it, lest you die." But the serpent said to the woman, "You will not surely die."

Did you see what he did? He cast doubt on what Eve believed to be true. But then Eve chose to believe Satan. That is why we pray to know God better and seek help with protecting against our unbelief. It matters not that we accept the gift. It matters that we believe in the reason for the gift and the giver of it.

Just a Thought…

23
I Am Mature in Christ

I am mature in Christ and I am no longer an infant. I know this to be true for I have learned all this through walking with and experiencing God over the last 32 years. I no longer can lay claim to a lack of knowledge of God, but only a lack of submission to Him. For I know now that faith is a redirecting of my sight, a getting out of the focus of my own vision and getting God into focus. It is not faith in me through Christ, but rather faith in Christ period. I don't need to produce faith in me for that is not the goal.

I am able to say with confidence that….

I believe that God is who He says He is.
I believe that Jesus died for my sins to reconcile me before God.
I believe that I will be with God in all eternity.
I believe in God's provision.
I believe that God has overcome the world.
I believe in all of God's ways.
I believe He can and will restore my sanity.
I believe God is good and only good can come from Him for He is without sin.
I believe God asks me to work but not to worry.
I believe God will guide my steps if I submit to Him.
I know the pathway to God.
I can do all things through Christ who strengthens me. Apart from Jesus, I can do nothing.
That I am in desperate need of a savior.
That God never leaves me or has ever forsaken me and is faithful.
That God's ways are only good and always best for me.
That I am forgiven.
That He is still working in my life.
That I am truly wretched and self-centered.
That I need God daily.
That He provides for me and protects me.
That by creation alone I know Him.
That all I desire is grace.
That His word is the truth.
That I can't even begin to imagine all He can do.

That even my breath in my lungs is His.
That He has made this day and every day.
That I am loved by God.
There is power in prayer.
That He died for the sin that I did yesterday, the ones that I will do today, and the ones that I will do tomorrow.
That nothing in this world can separate me from God's love.
That each day His mercies are new.
That trouble will come to me. I don't have to go looking for it and yet, Christ has overcome all the trouble in the world.
That when I give, I receive more.
When I trust God, I feel His peace.
I know that God is always present with me .
That God is faithful and just.
There is no condemnation that comes from God.
That He works all things for good according to His purpose in my life and those who love Him.
That His ways are always, 100% of the time, better than mine.
I do not understand everything and do not need to.
The fruits of the spirit are my guide to the condition of my heart.
That God does not care what I do for a living, but only cares about the condition of my heart, for He knows when this is right, whatever I do, it will be to glorify Him.

Today, 32 years after accepting Jesus as my savior, I am grateful for His continued work in my life, transforming me into His likeness. As I mature in Christ, I become less, and He becomes more.

Stop today long enough to ask yourself, what don't you already know about Jesus?

If you are at the beginning of your journey, then drink in all you can. Should you have walked with Him for a great length of time, then lay claim to what you know to be true.

1 Peter 2:2
² Like newborn babies, crave pure spiritual milk, so that by it you may grow up in your salvation.

1 Corinthians 14:20
[20] Brothers and sisters stop thinking like children. In regard to evil be infants, but in your thinking be adults.

Galatians 6:14
[14] May I never boast except in the cross of our Lord Jesus Christ, through which the world has been crucified to me, and I to the world.

Just a Thought…

24
If You Are...

Satan uses doubt as a key weapon to take us away from God. He said to Eve, "Did God actually say...?" And with Jesus, he said "If you are...?"

Satan was a fool to temp Jesus. However, we do the same thing when we say, "Jesus if you are truly God, then heal me, fix me, protect me, provide for me." We are putting Gods reputation to the test. We are saying only if you do these things on my command will I then believe you are who you say you are.

God, however, was and is always way ahead of us. He knows those are the things we will need from Him before we ever asked for them. He created us and by doing so, knows what we needed in this world. God knows that even if He would act upon our command and deliver all we ask, we would still come up short. For what we ask for, only feeds our selfishness and not a deeper, much more fulfilling need that is to die to ourselves and to love him and his people.

The transition for a human to go from self-centeredness to selflessness is the path less traveled. How many of us are willing to tempt God and say, "If you are truly God then, take away all my selfish desires, my power, my possessions, my money, my time, my heart, and use it to serve you, Lord, and your people."?

Now that is a temptation, I think God would honor! It would bring God the greatest joy to show you His transforming powers, that you would be aligned with His purpose.

The great news is even here, we don't need to tempt God. He provided this as well with the death of Jesus. He has nothing that He needs to prove or that we can tempt Him by. He has given us everything we could ever want or need. The choice is to believe or not. It's not a matter of Him performing, it's a matter of us believing in His performance.

The question to put before God is not, "If you are…" rather, it is, "Will you…?" Will you forgive me? Will you help me with my unbelief? Will you guide me onto your paths? Will you teach me to love like you do?

So, as God works in us, we will go from "If you are…?" to "I know you are…!"

Just a Thought…

25
It's All Good

Think back to when you were young. It's a Saturday. You would wake up and think, what a great day; no school and you get to go over to Johnny's house and play all day.

His house was great. He had a swimming pool in the backyard, all the latest video games, tons of food in the fridge. He loved to play sports as much as you did. The two of you would talk and laugh all day. It was going to be a great day…guaranteed. You could hardly wait to get out of bed and get dressed and run over there.

The same is true with God. Scripture tells us:

Psalm 118:24
[24] *The Lord has done it this very day; let us rejoice today and be glad.*

What does a day look like that God made? What comes to your mind?

God has all the creativity, resources, power, and strength to do what He wants this day.

One thing we must take into consideration is that, God can do only good. Nothing can come from Him that is not good for us or Him.

We, on the other hand, can create very little and have limited access to resources, power, and strength and at best, can randomly do good. Our sinful nature will play tricks on us and let us think we are doing good, when in our hearts we know our selfishness, fear, pride, greed, insecurity, and ego are what's driving us.

So, God asks us to come to His house today and play, to join Him in what He planned to do. He guarantees it will be good. He says leave all your stuff at home and come on over. Just bring yourself.

He has everything else covered! It's Saturday every day at His house.

Here is what you will get by hanging with God.

Galatians 5:22-23
²² But the fruit of the Spirit is love, joy, peace, forbearance, kindness, goodness, faithfulness, ²³ gentleness and self-control. Against such things there is no law.

Furthermore, it is impossible to know what the day will truly be for.

1 Corinthians 2:9
⁹ However, as it is written:
"What no eye has seen,
    what no ear has heard,
and what no human mind has conceived"[a] —
    the things God has prepared for those who love him —

So, get up, get dressed, and head on over to God's house today and join Him in what He is doing. It's all Good! Guaranteed!

Just a Thought…

26
As a Man Believes

The saying goes, "As a man thinketh, so goes he."

I contend that we can think all we want to never end up going in that direction. Take procrastination as an example. We think we want to go in a certain way, but never end up there. Thinking takes the energy of the mind. Believing, on the other hand, takes from the mind but also the heart, body, and soul.

That is why, in John 3:16 God says, 'Those who believe in his Sons' death will be saved. Not those who think about it." Going from thinking to believing is a gap as small as that hair on your head to as wide as the Grand Canyon. In either case, it takes an action of the will to cross over. You can't think your way over. You must actively surrender your emotions, your fears, your desires and die to yourself.

Oswald Chambers in his book *My Utmost for His Highest* says, "Either you live and God dies within you or God lives and you die."

Going from thinking to believing takes more focused thought and emotion. You will find an internal anxiousness within your soul. This happens not just in spiritual realms but anytime you chose to believe something that contradicts your way of being.

Should a person sincerely want to change their life, it will take much more than positive thinking or self-talk.

In Romans you see where Abraham became fully convinced. He went from thinking to believing in the fact that God keeps his promises.

Romans 4:21
[21] *being fully persuaded that God had power to do what he had promised.*

How did he do this?

Romans 4:20
[20] Yet he did not waver through unbelief regarding the promise of God, but was strengthened in his faith and gave glory to God,

He grew into it. His faith grew by experiencing God and seeing His promises fulfilled to a point where he could say, "Enough already, I believe you will keep your promises from here on out."

We too just don't jump into a belief. We must test the water, research its merits before we take the leap. But there is no way around the fact that there will be a point where we surrender and choose to believe. That time frame is different for everyone, but the results are the same.

So, when we look at our life, past, present, and future, rather than assess our thinking, it is better to take inventory of our beliefs.

As a man believes so goes, he.

Just a Thought…

27
He Made Me This Way

Romans 9:20
[20] But who are you, a human being, to talk back to God? "Shall what is formed say to the one who formed it, 'Why did you make me like this?'"

Lord, this is me, forgive me. I have said these hundreds of times. I say it out of frustration at my inability to stop sinning. When I sin, I get angry with you for my actions. I would say You know me Lord – why didn't You stop me? You made me this way. But I now know You didn't make me this way, for that would mean You made me a sinner, deceitful, lustful, hateful, prideful.

How could that be when You made me in Your image. For that would mean You were the same. You made me like You, loving, caring, kind, protective of those I love, fruitful, smart, patient, joyful, peaceful. That is who I am. I am not that other person. Those things I do, I hate, but beneath all the bad, You made me good.

It's not a matter of me shaking my fist at You out of anger for making me. It is me crying out to You to help me be more like what You made me be and lean on You.

It is comforting to know that I'm already made like You. It's just peeling off the layers of sinfulness to get to the root of who I truly am.

I can see it, Lord. If I give You all my trust then I'm free to be who You made me, which is a manifestation of You. It's not miles away or a thousand layers deep. It is one prayer away every moment. It's knowing and no longer wondering or guessing where or what the path back home is. The path has a bright shining light on it in the middle of darkness. It's one step in front of me. No wall to climb, distance to walk, tunnel to dig. It's hidden no longer now that I believe in Jesus. It's not a degree of effort or level of expertise, it's not a position of power or financial status to reach.

I'm there, I'm just a simple prayer away. Nothing more.

Lord, help me back on the path for I went astray. You never say no. You never remind me of my sin, You never punish me, or condemn me. You simply reach out Your hand and place me back on the path. We start walking again without any guilt or shame. Just a walk, God and His child who is made in his image. Oh, how beautiful the walk is. It's everything and more than I ever could have imagined. There is a peace that transcends understanding, a love that is to the core of my soul, a compassion towards others without restraint. I see all things through Your eyes, Lord. My heart breaks for what breaks Yours. I long to want to help others. I no longer have to worry, for my life is in Your hands.

You walk through this dark world bright shining as the sun. I have not lost days for today is a new day. I can awake with great anticipation and not fear. Though trials keep coming, as You said they would, I do not ever have to leave the path again. I can do anything now through Your strength within me. I'm made in Your image and heir to Your kingdom as Your child. I don't boast or become anything other than what will glorify You.

Lord, I lay my fist down and raise my hands to You for making me this way, in your image. I hear You say "Welcome home son! Let's go for a walk!"

Just a Thought…

28
Enduring Joy

Hebrews 12:2
² fixing our eyes on Jesus, the pioneer and perfecter of faith. For the joy set before him, he endured the cross, scorning its shame, and sat down at the right hand of the throne of God.

What was this joy that was set before Him that gave Him enough strength to endure being crucified? What did He see?

He saw that His children would be forgiven of their sins forever.
He saw that He had a way in which His children could be reunited with Him.
He saw how His children could be free once again of religion.
He saw how the hearts of His children could be filled.
He saw Satan being defeated once and for all.
He saw the relationship with His children being restored.
He saw the end of time on earth for everything was leading up to this day, and it was on this day that He will prove that He was the Son of God and that His father would be glorified.

If He could endure such pain for us with a joy-filled heart, what joy can we find when we deny ourselves in order to glorify Him?

Just a Thought…

29
Two Worlds

We live in two worlds: the spiritual and the secular. If you give it some thought, it will become clear. Each day we go about doing things of this world. We eat, dress, work, entertain, socialize, explore, and have recreation. Yet, in the midst of this world, we are drawn to prayer, worship, church, and serving all in relationship with God. The two worlds have a mighty force that competes like a game of tug and war.

So, we determine that life is meant to be this way. Living in two distinct worlds. How exhausting this becomes. At the end of each day, we have battle fatigue. Yet there is one unique difference. When we choose to live in the spiritual world, we are called to go into the secular world and bring the gifts of the spirit. This is bringing God's kingdom and will to be done on earth as it is heaven. Should we choose to live in the secular world, we will be drawn away from the spiritual world, never to return. This living takes from us and is designed only to satisfy the self.

God wants us to be of one mind. The only way to combine the two worlds into one is through submitting to God. We can be a light into darkness, peace in the midst of crisis, support to the worried, comfort to those are suffering and joy to those who are in sorrow.

We are in this world but not of this world.

Just a Thought…

30
The Ask

Ephesians 3:20
²⁰ Now to him who is able to do immeasurably more than all we ask or imagine, according to his power that is at work within us,

When we pray, we ask God for something – be it peace, or love or understanding. It might be healing or comfort, maybe something tangible, like money, a job, transportation. Nonetheless, we are only able to ask for something that we can imagine, which is limited to our own human understanding. God says He is able and will do more than we can ask or imagine. Couple this with knowing that God only has our best interest in mind and His ultimate plan before Him, it appears that we should pray only that His will, not ours be done.

Why would anyone want to limit God to answer a prayer that is bound by our limited imagination? If we knew all the choices truly available to us, perhaps we would have prayed for something different on the list.

Consider a prayer that would be like this:

God, I pray Your will be done today in my life and around the world. I know Your ways are higher and better than I could ever imagine. I desire that You will be glorified and believe that You know what is best for me today. With your strength, I will follow You and trust You, for You have been faithful. I will go about my day with my eyes set upon You and will follow You wherever You want me to go.

In Jesus' name!

Amen.

Just A Thought…

31

Being Known

"All social interchange between human beings is a response of personality to personality; grading upward from the most casual brush between man and man to the fullest, most intimate communion of which the human spirit is capable. Religion, so far as it is genuine, is in essence the response of created personalities to the creating personality, God. And this is life eternal, that they might know thee the only true God and Jesus Christ, whom thou hast sent." – Book: The Pursuit of God. AW Tozer

Who are you in the deepest relationship with? Who knows you the best of anyone, your most inner thoughts, your deepest emotions, your worst fears, your passions, longings, desires? And in truth, do they really know everything about you? Are there things about you that you have not shared for you are still after all these years withholding while building trust?

Do we realize that upon each step toward another person, yielding our personality, we build deepening relationships that can last a lifetime? The speed by which this develops is totally up to the two parties choosing to be vulnerable. However, with God, it is different. For He knows us better than we know ourselves. Nothing is hidden from Him. He starts at the end of the relationship by immediately giving us His entire love and being. He withholds nothing. The relationship only grows by our willingness to spend time with Him, to know that He knows our fears, sins, pain, inadequacy and sadness. He also knows what we need to experience love, joy and peace.

He removes the need to earn His love, to justify or manipulate our way with Him. He gives us space and is not smothering yet always longs to be with us . Although the relationship can never be equal in nature, He never lords his divinity over us yet protects us, provides for us and comforts us.

Think about the gap between the level of being known by your closest relationships and being known by God. Man, at best, can know another to the level of their own vulnerability and capacity which can never match up to that of God's.

Draw near to God and yet know it's not a matter of Him knowing you, it is a matter of you getting to know Him. Talk with Him about who He is, what He likes, what His plans are, His hopes and dreams. Ask Him what He likes to do, what breaks His heart, and what brings Him joy. Think of ways of celebrating with Him on key days like Easter and Christmas and mourn with Him on Good Friday.

Pick up His book and read about him. Sing songs to Him. Write Him letters and go for casual walks or just hang out with Him and enjoy the sunset.

Get to know Him.

Just a Thought…

32
From God's Seat

I sit in my chair and list my prayers giving them to God. I then think of the hundreds of millions of other people all doing the same today; prayers about family, health, financial, relationships, etc. I stopped to think about God receiving all these prayers and diligently trying to answer each one. Heal this person, find employment for that person, fix this relationship. On and on it goes.

God knows that if He were to grant all prayers today that tomorrow because of our sinfulness, we would create a whole new set of problems to pray for. Although God can and does at times answer surface prayers, He tells us how to go beyond these matters to reach the richest answer to prayers which are love, peace, compassion, contentment, and ultimately eternal life.

He even went to the extent of sending Jesus to die for the sins behind these prayers to remove them forever.

God, you truly do know us and love us.

Read God's promises, find where He come up short? I dare you!

Just a Thought…

33
The Right-Hand Man

Isaiah 41:13
¹³ For I am the Lord your God
 who takes hold of your right hand
and says to you, Do not fear;
 I will help you.

When I was six months old, I contracted polio. There was no vaccine when I was first diagnosed in 1954. The disease spread to both my arms, legs and my neck. Later in the year, the vaccine was released. The cure was a miracle and it went on to heal all my limbs and neck except my right arm. This remained damaged. I would never have use of the arm again.

Growing up, this became a burden that affected my life not only physically, but emotionally. Learning to function in the world took training by my parents, who were truly amazing. I was taught how to dress myself, cut my food, tie my shoes. I was taught how to play sports. I even made the high school baseball team. What my parents couldn't do for me, what I had to learn myself, was how to interact with people and their perception of me. This would become a daily battle for the rest of my life. My right arm became my weak point.

When reading this verse where God says He will take me by my right hand, I felt Him saying I will take hold of your weakness. Do not be afraid, I will help you. He was able to find the area in my life that had the most impact and give me comfort. I know it's more of a metaphor hat His words and my right hand happen to match up, but I feel He is saying to everyone that, 'I know your weakest point, the area where you need the most comfort.'

Is it a physical problem, emotional, financial, relational one? Is it your sinful past or current betrayal? Could it be an addiction or maybe abuse? Whatever it is, He will take hold of it and ask you to trust Him and not to fear – to walk confidently into this new day.

I also found it interesting that in this scripture, God is proactive and reaches out and takes your hand. He knows in those weakest areas of our life, we need Him to step towards us. Where most people in the world shy away from helping others in their weakness, God finds it His joy.

Just a Thought…

34
Slavery is Still Alive

Romans 6:16
¹⁶ Don't you know that when you offer yourselves to someone as obedient slaves, you are slaves of the one you obey—whether you are slaves to sin, which leads to death, or to obedience, which leads to righteousness?

When talking about slavery, we cringe at the memories of our African-American brothers and sisters who were treated with such ugliness. When we read about today's modern-day slavery, we label human trafficking, we burn with anger. Yet, we seldom look at sin as our captive owner and that we would call ourselves slaves. We pride ourselves, even go to war for our freedom.

In the quietness of our soul, we find ourselves battling things such as alcohol, drugs, sex, food, codependency, work, spending, power, hatred, resentment, jealousy, envy, and greed that enslave our bodies, minds, and souls. Yet we refuse to accept that we are SLAVES.

What we don't realize is the root of slavery lies in one or more of these internal sins that control us. There can be no outward sin without an internal sin, which manifests itself externally. Only hatred, power, and greed could ever cause a person to convince themselves they have a right to own another human being.

Paul tells us to be aware of this battle within, to turn the battle over to Christ to fight.

2 Corinthians 10:5
⁵ We demolish arguments and every pretension that sets itself up against the knowledge of God, and we take captive every thought to make it obedient to Christ.

And by doing so, he will provide a way out.

1 Corinthians 10:13
¹³ No temptation has overtaken you except what is common to mankind. And God is faithful; he will not let you be tempted beyond what you can bear. But when you are tempted, he will also provide a way out so that you can endure it.

Yet there is one step – the most important step we are responsible for, and that is to…

"Admit that you, yourself, are powerless to overcome your addictions and that your life has become unmanageable."

Let's abolish slavery once and for all. Each time we admit to God that we need Him, we establish and take hold of our true freedom. When we are free, we then can help free others.

Just a Thought…

35
Nice Try, Satan

Hebrews 12:2
²fixing our eyes on Jesus, the pioneer and perfecter of faith. For the joy set before him *he endured the cross, scorning its shame, and sat down at the right hand of the throne of God.*

I can imagine Jesus sitting on the throne next to God looking down on earth and speaking to Satan saying, "Nice try Satan. You gave it your best but, in the end, it was not enough. You…
Tried to tempt me to turn away from God
Had people mock me
Had people betray me
Had people insult me
Had people spit on me
Had people whip me
Had people place a crown of thorns on my head
Had people lie to me
Even had people crucify me
Yet in the end, through the power of my Father, I endured it all. There is nothing that you could ever do that I can't overcome.

Now, with all the power given to me by my father, I too, give to all those that believe in me, so they also will overcome all that you try and tempt them with. You have been rendered powerless over them even to death, for they will rise again and live with us in heaven for all of eternity. You have been defeated!

For those who believe…
For every temptation – I will provide a way out.
For every pain – I will provide comfort.
For every loss – I will come near.
For every sacrifice – I will replenish tenfold.
For every betrayal – I will be faithful.
For every fear or worry – I will give my peace.
For every sickness – I will ultimately heal.
For every death – I give eternal life.

The very best you can do is to temporarily distract my people. Yet I give them churches to attend, bible studies to join, my bible to read, songs to sing, creation to contemplate, and direct access to me through prayer to keep them on track. Oh, but the best yet is that I left my Holy Spirit in them when I left this earth, so they have a 24/7, 365-day-a-year helper to guide them.

You see Satan, it's time you concede, but I know you too well. You won't. So, the day is coming that I will return and once and for all you will be eliminated, and my Father's plan will be completed.

Nice try Satan, but you lose!

Just a Thought…

36
Break My Heart

Lord, break my heart today for what breaks Yours.

What are those things that breaks Gods heart? If you're a parent, what things break your heart when you watch your children grow up? When you watch the news, what things do you see that breaks your heart? I can only imagine what God feels when He sees His children…

Worrying about the little things in life
That are full of anger
That cheat another person
That lie to one another
That steal from each other
That curse and especially when they use His Son's name
That are selfish
That are greedy
That oppress others by their abuse of power
That destroy His creation
That are starving
That are homeless
That are single moms
Those that don't believe and will be separated from Him for eternity
A widow that's all alone
Christians that fight with one another
Go to war with each other
That have been murdered
That have been raped
That are fighting an addiction
That have been caught up in human trafficking
That practice or participate in prostitution
That are depressed and insecure
That lost a loved one
A pastor who falls to temptation
Those who are a part of a Church that closes its doors to the lost
That are going through a divorce
That are being physically abused

That don't trust Him
That don't love Him and love another god
That are struck with a debilitating disease

Lord, the more I think about it as I think about it, I would imagine the rain from above are the tears from Your eyes, as You weep over these things. The sadness is from the frustration You feel that You must refrain Yourself from using the almighty power You embody to just snap your fingers and remove all the pain and agony You observe and to know that your children are only a prayer away from receiving You in their life and how You can then guide them through life's trials.

Lord, amid any one of these trials, we can turn toward You and receive Your peace and strength. By doing so, we can then help our brother or sister do the same.

I again can only imagine how God feels when He hears His children say, "Lord, break my heart for what breaks Yours and use me today to make this world a better place."

Maybe the ray of sunshine that breaks through the cloudy day is truly the radiance from your smile.

Just a Thought…

37
Which Is Harder?

Matthew 11:28-30
²⁸ "Come to me, all you who are weary and burdened, and I will give you rest. ²⁹ Take my yoke upon you and learn from me, for I am gentle and humble in heart, and you will find rest for your souls. ³⁰ For my yoke is easy and my burden is light."

Have you heard someone say, "Following God sure is hard work?" I ask you – which is harder: to live in this world with God or without Him?

To walk in this world, one will face all that it has to offer. There are many good things we can enjoy, such as sunny days with blue skies, white sandy beaches, snow-covered mountain tops, the birth of a child, the union of a marriage, the victory of your favorite sports team, the pride in your child's accomplishment, the discovery of new places, or the soothing sound of a sweet melody. Yet, there is the ugly side of life that carries with its hatred, murder, rape, lust, greed, racism, oppression, addiction, disease, terrorism, and deep sadness. It seems at times, darkness outweighs the good. That is why it takes great strength to rise up and see the beauty in the moment.

When left to our own strength, walking without God, we become weary and heavy burdened. We collapse, concede, and yield to the darkness. We lose hope and many times give up.

When walking with God, the world as we know still exists with all it's good and bad.

Yet God says, "When the bad comes, hold tight to my hand and I will give you peace and joy during it. I will take on all the weight the darkness sends your way. All you must do is to believe. So, when the good of the world is in your sights, just praise me and when darkness comes, trust me and goodness will prevail."

So, which is harder to face? This world without God or to believe in the One who overcame the world, which He will guide you through?

You decide.

Just a Thought…

38
It's Not All Bad

I'm sure you have heard someone say, "Why do bad things happen to good people?" Maybe you found yourself asking the same question as you observe life around you. I, too, ask this question as I read the email saying our pastor is in the hospital because of a heart attack.

We then try to lean on *Romans 8:28*
[28] *And we know that in all things God works for the good of those who love him, who have been called according to his purpose.*

Good and suffering seem to me to be like oil and water trying to mix together when they never could blend. Yet, we have seen great good come to the very depths of experiencing even the most extreme trials. We even assign words such as hero, heroic, amazing, unbelievable, courageous, sacrifice, love, strong, perseverance, and even miracle when we observe good during trials.

We all have wrestled with the understanding of God when we try to reconcile bad things happening to good people. We question His love, His character, His power, and His authority. We even go as far as blaming and shaking our fist towards Him. Yet, who will be the first to comfort God when He watches from above all the hurt, the pain, that His children cause each other or the abuse of His beautiful creation to serve the greed within His children's hearts, or the mere fact that He had to sacrifice His Son on a cross after being beaten, rejected, mocked, and spit on all in order that we may be saved from punishment for what we justly created on our own?

God's most extreme decision was to find a way that good would overcome bad forever. He took the ultimate good person who had walked the earth and subjected Him to the most excruciating pain and ultimate death so that once and for all, good would prevail for all His children forever.

We have difficulty seeing the good when during trials, yet we can know that it is there to be discovered. Bad things happen to all people, both those we label good or bad. We must choose to believe that good wins in the end, every time. If not, then Jesus' death was for nothing.

So why did a bad thing happen to such a good person?

Just a Thought…

39
Don't Need to Come

Have you ever wondered why, if God says He is always with us and He will never leave or forget us that we pray for His presence?

In the fictional book, *The Shack* by William Young, there was a quote that God made to the main character, Mack, that got me thinking. "Mack, the reason you face fears and anxiety about the future is that you fail to see that I am there with you."

When I say the word "future" how far out from the present moment does your mind immediately take you? Two minutes, two days, a week, a month, ten years? Yet, if God is always with us, where and how we sense that he left is when we think about the future? Did we lose or misplace Him?

If we are experiencing God in the moment, what changed when we entered the very next moment that causes us to pray for God to return? He never left and physically we never left as it is our body that transports us through each moment. Therefore, the only thing that left was our minds. Our thoughts left the present moment in order to live in the future or the past.

If given the chance to think about the fact that God is with you today and will be with you every second after that into eternity, you will find an unexplainable peace. You no longer have to look for God. You no longer need to pray for Him to draw closer or for Him to enter the room with you. Your prayers will always be, "Lord, help me see, feel, touch or hear Your presence."

When I now see into the future, I have to tell myself that if Jesus is with me now and is delivering me through today's trials, He will be with me in the same way at that future time and place. So, there is no need to worry, as Jesus and I will deal with it when that moment truly comes. This frees me up to stay in the present moment with Him. This took nothing on my part but to stop and think about it. God did the rest.

Psalm 46:10
¹⁰ He says, "Be still, and know that I am God;
  I will be exalted among the nations,
  I will be exalted in the earth."

Just a Thought…

40
True or False

True or false? In your relationship with God answer these questions:

Do you dictate the terms of what is good or bad?
Do you dictate the terms of how you want to be loved?
Do you dictate the terms of what success is?
Do you dictate the terms of how you expect your life to turn out?
Do you determine what your God is to be like?
Do you determine what is a blessing or not?
Do you determine what you think you should have to make you happy?
Do you determine what you feel your fair share of this life should be?
Do you decide what is fair or not?
Do you determine what is truth or a lie?
Do you determine who you will love today?
Do you determine how much of your resources you will donate?
Do you determine what amount of love you are willing to show another person?
Do you choose how much of God you want each day?
Do you get to ignore all the truth about healthy living and expect to that you will never be ill?
Do you decide who is more important in a relationship?
Do you decide what is to be forgiven?

Once you have finished, add up all the "TRUES" and all the "FALSES". Determine what the percent of the total for each one is. When done, ask yourself one more question. Who is in control of your life, you or God? What percent?

If God seeks total control of your life, what areas do you feel you need to surrender over to Him?

Lord, hear our prayer.

Psalms 139:23-24
²³ Search me, God, and know my heart;
　test me and know my anxious thoughts.
²⁴ See if there is any offensive way in me,
　and lead me in the way everlasting.

Just a Thought…

41
This is the Day

Psalm 118: 24
The Lord has done it this very day;
  let us rejoice today and be glad.

Have you ever planned a party or event for someone else's benefit, maybe a birthday party, farewell gathering, baby shower, wedding, surprise party, anniversary, or celebration of an achievement? How long did it take you? How much did it cost you? How many ideas and thoughts went through your head to think of ways that the day will be truly special for that one person? How many others did you recruit to help you out?

Given some thought, I sense you will remember, for that period of time leading up to the event, that your mind was preoccupied with the person you wanted to bring joy to and you imagined, multiple times, their reaction as being one of rejoicing, gratefulness, of feeling honored and in amazement that you would go through the effort you did to make sure their day was one to remember.

When God asks us to rejoice in this day that He has made for us, He too, has given this day some prior thought with us in mind. He gave us miracles every day for our pleasure that we now just come to expect. Things like the sun rising or breath in our lungs. Yet, beyond the thousands of daily miracles that we walk by, God still finds new ways for us to rejoice in the day He made for us. I'm not talking about parting-the-sea type miracles, but rather subtle ones like feeling His presence, leaning on His faithfulness, or experiencing His miraculous peace amid turmoil. When God asks us to rejoice in the day He has made, He is asking us to slow down and take in the entire day and all it has to offer.

When our guest of honor shows up at the event, we made for them, we too, want them to look around and notice the decorations, the food, the people, the music, and the joy in the room. Would you agree that the greatest gift you can give to the host of the event in your honor would be to enjoy it? Let the host see your laughter and smile and that you are having a great time. Then, when it's over, let the host know how grateful you were for them planning this event.

I heard someone say the best way to show God that you love him is to believe that He really loves you.

When our guest finishes their day, if we knew without a doubt they felt loved because of the event, then we will be well-pleased. Let God know that not only was this day worth rejoicing for, but even more so that you know He did all this for you because He loves you.

Just a Thought…

42
I Can't Get No Satisfaction

"There are some advantages to being God. By nature, I am completely unlimited, without bounds. I have always known fullness. I live in a state of perpetual satisfaction as my normal state of existence." – The Shack, William Young

Have you ever been satisfied? Defined as "the contentment one feels when one has fulfilled a desire, need, or expectation". If you have, how long did you stay there? Seconds, minutes, days? Can you remember what that felt like? Would you describe it as being done, finished, complete, happy, content, peaceful, fulfilled? There is that feeling that you no longer have any need to pursue reaching that goal, resolving that issue, reconciling that relationship, or finishing that project. You are done.

Some may say that being satisfied means a person lacks motivation, initiative, a striving for more or better. How do you look at a person who claims they are satisfied right where they are at? I imagine that you subconsciously begin to judge, assessing their sense of completion against yours. Take, for example, someone says that they are satisfied turning in what you would consider a "C" level work. You can tell they sincerely are content, and you see no angst in them. What is going through your mind at that moment? Might you be questioning that person by saying to yourself, "What gives them the right to turn this assignment in like this and feel it's okay? There is so much more that could or should have been done." Or, I would never do that. Doesn't he or she take any pride in their work?

If you were perpetually satisfied, does that sound peaceful or boring?

I would propose that it's a desired but uncomfortable feeling. I think that deep down, we all want to reach that final button to hit at the finish line and say we are done. Yet, we keep hearing a whisper that says you're still not good enough. How dare you turn in this or that as a final assessment of your life!

I think there is another side of satisfaction that we have not seen this side of heaven.

I believe that satisfaction would be what it would feel like to truly stop and smell those roses forever. And going from rose to rose, sunset to sunrise, not wanting more but enjoying wherever you are at. No hurry, no competition, no comparison, no judgment, no hoarding, no sense of lacking, just being present to the moment and each moment thereafter.

Try today to find satisfaction in something, then stay there as long as you can, taking in everything about that moment and registering it deep inside your mind and soul. My guess is, you will find a smile on your face, but that it won't be long before you are convinced you must keep moving.

Ecclesiastes 2:24
24 A person can do nothing better than to eat and drink and find satisfaction in their own toil. This too, I see, is from the hand of God,

Just a Thought…

43
A Little Work Plus a Little Faith

Romans 3:27-28
²⁷ Where, then, is boasting? It is excluded. Because of what law? The law that requires works? No, because of the law that requires faith. ²⁸ For we maintain that a person is justified by faith apart from the works of the law.

Have you given it much thought to how you justify your belief in God?

If you had a scale and on one side you put in the good works you do, like going to church, reading your bible, praying, being kind and generous, telling the truth, donating to charity, etc. Then on the other side you put in faith, your full belief, devotion, trust, your heart, body, mind, and soul. How would it look?

Take a step back and look at the scale. Is it leaning to one side or the other? What would you say, 70% faith and 30% works or maybe 60% works and 40% faith? Maybe it is equally balanced. You know, just the right amount of work and faith?

Paul would say the scale is tipped 100% faith and 0% works when it comes to our belief in God. Let's not confuse the scripture where James ties faith and works together.

James 2:26
²⁶ As the body without the spirit is dead, so faith without deeds is dead.

There is a subtle difference when we look at faith and work. It boils down to the matter of the heart. The question resides in the motive of the heart. Is it love or performance?

In business, there is a big push for companies to determine their "WHY"; why they are doing what they are doing. The truly great companies start with their WHY, whereas, mediocre companies start with their "WHAT" they are doing. Can you see the heart in this analogy? God does not want our WHAT, He wants our WHY.

He knows when we lead with our WHY, the WHAT always follows.

Faith is about our WHY. We believe in God because we love Him. We finally came to the point in our life where our WHAT we were doing betrayed us, left us crushed in spirit. We love God because we now know we can't do it on our own and we need someone to rescue us. There is nothing left of our performing that works anymore. We are stripped to our core. Down on our knees, we come to Jesus broken, empty, and ready to believe. This is true faith.

In that moment, the scale is tipped 100% to faith. There is not one thing that you can put on the performance side of the scale that will help. On the contrary, until the scale is fully tipped towards faith, we won't receive what God has to offer. There can't be a trace of performance that we may be tempted to boast of our efforts.

Ephesians 2:8-9
8 For it is by grace you have been saved, through faith—and this is not from yourselves, it is the gift of God— 9 not by works, so that no one can boast.

Imagine for a minute that if works were the criteria for faith and for earning God's favor, then only the strong, with a high IQ and was wealthy could truly compete for their good work and could be measured. Maybe by quantity? The better sales number or better strategy could get the edge. I don't know about you, but in this scheme of things, I give up. I don't see me winning anything.

Once we have found true faith in Christ, performance takes on a whole new meaning. It will be impossible to receive the forgiveness of Christ without being changed on the inside. This change will drive your works going forward. It will be compassion, love, and gratitude that is behind your works. No longer will it be to earn favor, but rather a heart's desire to serve others for what God has done for you. So, when Paul says faith without work is dead, he means that those who claim to love Jesus and there is no sign of loving works, then faith must be dead.

It's my belief that at the very beginning of our faith journey, the scale is tipped fully in favor of faith. However, once we receive Christ through our faith journey, from that point forward until we die, will be God working through us to tip the scale to do His works – that someday, because of our faith, the scale will be 100% tipped toward His work. A little secret…do not try to add your selfish works to the scale thinking you help God a little to hurry up His goal.

Ask yourself today, why are you performing? Is it to earn something or someone's favor or because you love God and Him doing His works through you?

Just a Thought…

44
Forgiven

Psalms 32:1
¹ Blessed is the one
  whose transgressions are forgiven,
  whose sins are covered.

How important is it for you to be forgiven for something you know you have done wrong? There is a thing that can kill a person other than using weapons, diseases, and external forces and that is guilt! Guilt has been known to cause suicides.

Why would a pure emotion have the ability to drive a person to take their own life? After all, can't we just shake the feeling until it goes away? Guilt has been tied not just to suicide, but to murder, insanity, depression, overeating, divorce, homelessness, addiction, and many more disorders.

Why does guilt have such a strong impact on our lives? Are you experiencing guilt? How long have you been carrying this with you? Has it had any impact on your life, physically, emotionally or relationally? Guilt left unchecked will grow exponentially. Ask any addict after each time they pick up a drink or drug or watch pornography when they told themselves that morning, they would never do this again. Each time they fail, guilt increases and in order to medicate the pain, they must increase the quantity of the very thing they are addicted to. Unfortunately, this formula never works for them. It only works when they put a stop to doing what they are doing altogether. They will have to fight off many demons to do this, the very first one is guilt and the ability to admit they are powerless to stop on their own.

Blessed are those who are forgiven!

Have you ever been forgiven and afterward felt blessed, grateful, relieved, and freed at last? Once forgiven, you can then move forward and begin living your life again. Now hope, compassion, and joy reenter your life. Something happens to your heart that transforms your mind, body, and your soul.

Blessed are those who are forgiven!

Forgiveness is something that is given but only is benefited from when it is received.

It is something that must be asked for. Forgiveness impacts both the one giving it and the one receiving it independently and mutually inclusive. Yet the person doing the forgiving is not relieving guilt, but rather letting go of anger, resentment, and their need to be right. They, of course, receive their blessing by doing so. But to be forgiven, a person must accept it.

I can say I forgive so and so and sincerely be free yet, the other person can choose not to accept it and be left with all the trappings that have haunted them. Do we need God's forgiveness? If each person would forgive one another, wouldn't this wipe out any further need for forgiveness? Won't we be at peace?

When we sin, it results in guilt and the need for forgiveness, the sin was not just against the other person, it was against God. When we sin, we choose to turn away from God. Like the drug the addict takes is not the issue, but rather it's the manifestation of the negative emotion that is causing them to take the drug. The drug itself, if not consumed, has no power. The actual sin we perform is not the issue. It's the matter of the heart that caused us to sin – that's where the problem lies. This is where we choose to turn away from God.

Yes, we can feel free from accepting forgiveness from another person, yet still be at unrest until we reconcile with God. The power of God's forgiveness is much greater than man's.

Let's say you ask for forgiveness from the other person and they choose not to give it. Where does that leave you? How do you ever get freed from the guilt you feel?

When you receive God's forgiveness, it can free you regardless if the other person does or not. (Note that God will nudge you to seek forgiveness from the other person by admitting your wrongdoing, but He does not make you responsible for their response.)

Blessed are those who are forgiven!

I ask you to consider what carrying guilt has cost you in your life! If you are honest with yourself, you can quantify it. Add up the sleepless hours, trips to the therapists, the broken relationships, money spent medicating, loss of health, and missed opportunities to enjoy life. If you are truly honest with yourself, you will feel a sense of envy and longing when you read the verse.

Psalms 32:1
[1] Blessed is the one
　whose transgressions are forgiven,
　whose sins are covered.

You're one prayer away from receiving God's blessing!

Just a Thought…

45
Take My Path

I AM WITH YOU AND FOR YOU.

"When you decide on a course of action that is in line with My will, nothing in heaven or on earth can stop you. You may encounter many obstacles as you move toward your goal. With My help, you can overcome any obstacle. Do not expect an easy path as you journey hand in hand with Me, but do remember that I, your very-present Helper, am omnipotent." – Sarah Young, Jesus Calling 1/9

Have you ever asked yourself, if God is omnipotent and I am doing His will, why do I have to face obstacles and troubles along the way? Why not clear sailing ahead?

Here is a test. If you were able to stand completely still for 24 hours, not adding or taking away anything from this world, then observe the world's activities around you, would they be filled with peace and quiet? Is your physical body at complete comfort and a sense of calm? What is happening with the weather around you? Depending on where you were standing, such as on a remote island or in the middle of a war zone, your answers will differ in detail. However, the one thing that is common regardless where you are standing is that throughout the 24 hours, your experience will be changing moment by moment.

Your physical body will be going through physical adjustments such as hunger, stiffness, unrest, cramping, heart rate fluctuation, and your mind will go through a thousand thoughts – ranging from peace to doubt to fear to joy and around and around it will go. The elements around you will change. Light and darkness will exchange hands, temperatures, air flow, smells, noises will all be fluctuating. Now throw other human beings in the mix that cross your path while you are doing nothing but standing still and watch what will happen. Early on, you will most likely just be passed by, but as the day goes on, people will begin noticing your lack of movement. Some may come up and stare. Some will ask questions to fulfill their curiosity. Some will be genuinely concerned, and some will see an opportunity to take advantage of you. There may be some who seek to taunt you and even inflict harm on you. Remember you have done nothing but stand there asking for and requiring nothing. I hope you can see by imagining you doing this exercise, the world around you will bring a variety of activity, good and bad, around you and within you.

One last part of the experiment. After the 24 hours are over, on the next 24 hours, I want you to start interacting with the world around you in any way you chose. Observe how and what affects you bring to the experiment. Will you bring joy and peace or greed and resentment? Will you bring expectations or pour out generosity? Will you judge or offer support? Will you be self-serving or look for opportunities to serve? Will you run and hide, or will you stand boldly? Every movement you take will have a ripple effect in the world.

Now back to the story. God is saying that when you follow Him, you will face obstacles and trials and suffering. But He will never leave you and He will give you the strength to endure and the heart to find peace and joy along the way.

The world will, by itself, generate problems along your path. God is just clearing the path before you. If you decide to run out in front of Him, you will face them on your own. If you walk behind Him it truly is clear sailing ahead. The key is to stay on His path, walk at His speed, and trust Him as He clears the way for you.

"Much, much stress results from your wanting to make things happen before their times have come. One of the main ways I assert My sovereignty is in the timing of events. If you want to stay close to Me and do things My way, ask Me to show you the path forward moment by moment. Instead of dashing headlong toward your goal, let Me set the pace. Slow down and enjoy the journey in My Presence" – Sarah Young, the remaining writing from 1/9 Jesus Calling entry.

Just a Thought...

46
Threshold

Romans 1:21-23
²¹ For although they knew God, they neither glorified him as God nor gave thanks to him, but their thinking became futile and their foolish hearts were darkened. ²² Although they claimed to be wise, they became fools ²³ and exchanged the glory of the immortal God for images made to look like a mortal human being and birds and animals and reptiles.

Do you know when you have reached your threshold? Everyone has one and everyone's is different. In fact, everyone moves the threshold at different levels depending on the decision they must make. I remember once I had a golden retriever that had hip dysplasia and required surgery, which was going to be very expensive. We didn't have much money then. When we heard the expense was over our financial threshold, we were forced to make a major decision. Feeling bad, I decided to ask around as to what other people's thresholds would be when spending money on medically treating a dog. I was very surprised that the numbers went from I would sell everything I had to help the dog to I would take the dog out back and shoot it to put it out of his misery (a little cold hearted).

We set thresholds for what we will pay for a car or a house or we set thresholds of time we will spend waiting for someone or for something to happen. We set thresholds for how much we want to learn or eat or exercise. We set thresholds for how far we will travel or how much we will give or if we will offer forgiveness. We also set thresholds for our belief in God.

The threshold seems to go up when things are going great, yet it goes down when things are not going so well. We say things like, 'God, why have you abandoned me or why did you allow for this to happen to me? You must not be a God I want to follow, so I will go and find another one.'

Paul was saying exactly that when he said to his listeners, "They exchanged the glory of the immortal God for images resembling mortal man and birds and animals and creeping things."

Where will you set your threshold for God when it comes to trusting Him? How much room are you giving Him to prove He is worthy of your time, talents, resources, and heart?

Every trial we go through will test the bar you set. Should you have trusted in Him, the bar will be raised higher, giving Him more room to work the next time. God asks that we remove the bar altogether when He said, "I will never leave you or forsake you. Be still and trust me for I have overcome the world. I will give you peace and depths of understanding which are beyond your ability. I will strengthen you in your weakness. I will give you purpose and a plan for your life. You will not fall for when things get hard, I will carry you. I am the same yesterday, today, and tomorrow. I am faithful until the very end, even to the extent of dying for you in order that you may truly live."

Remove the bar, give God full reign. When the bar is fully removed, you will be totally surrendered to His will and therefore, you will never again have to make the decision to cross the threshold or not.

Just a Thought…

47
Supreme Leadership

Hebrews 2:14-15
14 Since the children have flesh and blood, he too shared in their humanity so that by his death he might break the power of him who holds the power of death—that is, the devil—15 and free those who all their lives were held in slavery by their fear of death.

Have you ever noticed when leaders see a problem, they will delegate someone to do the task? When in reality it can only be best done by the leader themselves? When a corporation has lost its way and is off mission, the only one that can put it back on track is the leader. Yet, in order for the leader to be successful, they must get out from behind the desk, roll up their sleeves, and get dirty by going into the middle of the chaos.

God, who is the ultimate leader, knew this principle well. He looked down from heaven and saw that there was a severe problem with His organization. His people had turned against Him and each other. They had lost their way. All other efforts from the past were no longer working. There were seasons when things went well, but they never lasted very long. There was a root problem that had to be eliminated once and for all. No longer sending His angels to do the work, He Himself must do it.

Philippians 2:4-8
4 not looking to your own interests but each of you to the interests of the others.
5 In your relationships with one another, have the same mindset as Christ Jesus:
6 Who, being in very nature God,
   did not consider equality with God something to be used to his own advantage;
7 rather, he made himself nothing
   by taking the very nature of a servant,
   being made in human likeness.

> *⁸ And being found in appearance as a man,*
>   *he humbled himself*
>   *by becoming obedient to death—*
>   *even death on a cross!*

God went from sitting on the throne, to coming to earth, not as a king that everyone expected but rather in the humility, as He wanted His people to become. He knew in order to gain their trust He must get in the mix of things, get dirty, and feel and experience all that His people were facing. In doing this, He experienced physical pain, suffering, deep sorrow, abandonment, betrayal, temptation, ridicule, hatred, sadness, mourning, opposition, loneliness, and even to the extent of experiencing death. There was nothing He protected himself from.

Then in a way that only He could do, He rose from the dead, appeared to His people one last time to show that He has and will always overcome the ways of the world including death itself. Knowing that after every great presentation, in time, people will forget and lose their way again. He reached within Himself and gave His spirit to remain behind to be placed within the heart of those who would believe in the vision of the company to follow Him again. The spirit would be a forever personal trainer to help each person according to their need to protect them in the process.

Great leadership is only found in pure sacrifice of oneself for another. God is the model by which we must follow in order to lead well. He gave his life for the cause. What are you willing to give to further what you believe in?

Just a Thought…

48
You Asked for It

2 Chronicles 1:7-10
⁷ That night God appeared to Solomon and said to him, "Ask for whatever you want me to give you." ⁸ Solomon answered God, "You have shown great kindness to David my father and have made me king in his place. ⁹ Now, Lord God, let your promise to my father David be confirmed, for you have made me king over a people who are as numerous as the dust of the earth. ¹⁰ Give me wisdom and knowledge, that I may lead this people, for who is able to govern this great people of yours?"

Mark 10:51
⁵¹ "What do you want me to do for you?" Jesus asked him. The blind man said, "Rabbi, I want to see."

Have you ever thought how you would answer the question if God were to say to you, ask and it shall be given today to you? I can see your mind is churning, running through all the various choices, like a computer at top speed. Let's see some of the options:
Freedom to do whatever and whenever I want
Extreme wealth
Perfect health
Unbelievable talent
Never having to work again
Contentment
To find peace
To have joy
To be forgiven
To be loved
Sports car
A mansion
Disease healed
Handicap restored
A loving companion
Wisdom
Prophecy
Fame

Despite receiving any one of these wishes, history will tell us that we will still come up short. What is the one answer you can give that will prove to be the best choice? The answer would be to want whatever Jesus wants. To hand your gift of a free choice over to Jesus and let Him choose.

2 Chronicles 16:9
⁹ For the eyes of the Lord range throughout the earth to strengthen those whose hearts are fully committed to him. You have done a foolish thing, and from now on you will be at war."

The Lord is searching the entire world looking for one who seeks the will of God. The funny thing is that when we give our free will over to Jesus, He always chooses what is best for us anyway. Be ready to give your answer the next time Jesus poses the question.

Just a Thought…

49
Solomon's Second Chance

It took the wisest man ever to walk on earth years to find true wisdom.

You may remember that God offered to give King Solomon anything he wanted to ask for. Solomon chose wisdom. God made him the wisest of all mankind. Solomon wrote Ecclesiastes to summarize his pursuit of the meaning of life. He begins saying:

Ecclesiastes 1:2
2 "Meaningless! Meaningless!"
  says the Teacher.
"Utterly meaningless!
  Everything is meaningless."

It dawned on me as I read Ecclesiastes that by a simple change in wording, the book would have a totally different meaning. You will notice that in the entire book, except at the very end, Solomon used the word "I". His writing was about him trying to do for himself what only God could do him. He was on a mission to find the meaning of life and what will produce joy and fulfillment. He went on his adventure of trying everything one could imagine for he had no financial, physical, educational or political constraints. He emerged himself in reading, studying, drinking, music, lust, toys, projects, power, hard work, possessions, relationships, politics, gathering, etc. Look closely and you will see it was always I tried, I did, I am, I purchased, I achievement, I, I, I.

As you read the book, you get a bit disheartened yourself, for truth be told he busted your bubble. For you too were hoping and rooting for one of his efforts to hit the jackpot and be the answer to your quest. You began to ask yourself, 'Why bother with life itself for it is as Solomon puts it, meaningless?' Thanks to Solomon's journal of his quest, we do know how the book ends.

Ecclesiastes 12:13
¹³ Now all has been heard;
  here is the conclusion of the matter:
Fear God and keep his commandments,
  for this is the duty of all mankind.

Yes, Solomon realizes that our whole life is meaningless without God. But this is like a cliff hanger in a movie. Okay, I get it. Fear God follow His ways. But then what happens? The movie ends, and we go 'UGH!'

I think Solomon should have written a sequel to his book. Ecclesiastes revisited. It would have started out the same but had a different tempo to it.

"I, Solomon, the wisest man on earth wanted to find the meaning of life. I found that life only will be fulfilled by knowing God." Here comes the fun part. Wait for it.

By knowing God, I found that HE will....
Give me joy
Provide for me
Protect me
Bring me laughter
Take me on wild adventures
Bring me to mountain tops
Allow me to experience peace beyond my understanding
Teach me to dance
Teach me to write
Teach me to create
Teach me to build
Teach me to sing
Teach me to serve
Teach me to help
Teach me to play
Teach me to be still
Fill my heart until it overflows with joy
Remove any anxiety
Provide unlimited patience
Reveal colors in their brilliance

Show me ways
Rise me up above my enemies

Then Solomon would end. "I have surveyed life with God at the center and found it too meaningful!"

Just a Thought…

50
Getting Dressed

Ephesians 6:13-17
[13] Therefore put on the full armor of God, so that when the day of evil comes, you may be able to stand your ground, and after you have done everything, to stand. [14] Stand firm then, with the belt of truth buckled around your waist, with the breastplate of righteousness in place, [15] and with your feet fitted with the readiness that comes from the gospel of peace. [16] In addition to all this, take up the shield of faith, with which you can extinguish all the flaming arrows of the evil one. [17] Take the helmet of salvation and the sword of the Spirit, which is the word of God.

When you get up in the morning and are getting dressed, picking out your clothes for the day, what is the criteria you are using to make the decision about what you will wear? Maybe it's something along these lines:

What is the weather going to be like?
Is this business casual or formal business attire?
Is this a fund-raising event or a casual get together?
Am I meeting someone new or am I amongst friends?
How am I physically feeling today?
Am I dressing to impress?

Paul, in Ephesians, talks about giving thought to how we will dress for the day, as it relates to preparing our minds and hearts on that same day. Yet his choices are not based on fashion, but rather on security. He is suggesting we put on clothing for protection. You would not dress in your bathing suit to go out in below zero temperatures. You would wear protective clothing to fend off the cold. This would be a conscious decision on your part. Paul is telling us that every day, there is a battle going on of spiritual dimensions. Yet we choose to leave the house without dressing for battle. What would you call the person who ignores severe storm warnings? Foolish?

To ignore Paul's warning would also be considered foolish. We act surprised when we go about our day and feel battle fatigue from the temptations and negative conditions of the world, we live in. We leave ourselves vulnerable to the evil elements of the world when we leave our suit of armor in the closet back home. At times, we might be in a rush and only grab partial items of the suit of armor. Oh, we have the helmet of salvation but forget the belt of truth. Paul makes it clear we need the whole armor of God.

Knowing that the enemy will look for signs of weaknesses, Paul wants us to be fully prepared for battle with the mindset of victory.

As you reach for each piece of armor, you begin to notice your confidence level increases as well. Each piece reminds you of the power that is given us through Christ. Once fully dressed, we then grab our shield and sword and walk boldly into our day.

2 Corinthians 10:4-6
[4] The weapons we fight with are not the weapons of the world. On the contrary, they have divine power to demolish strongholds. [5] We demolish arguments and every pretension that sets itself up against the knowledge of God, and we take captive every thought to make it obedient to Christ. [6] And we will be ready to punish every act of disobedience, once your obedience is complete.

At the end of the day, the fruits of the spirit, love, joy, peace, patience, kindness, goodness and self-control will be our reward. Before you leave your house today, stand in front of the mirror one more time to see if you are missing anything?

Just a Thought...

51
Going from Here to There

Psalms 23:4
⁴ Even though I walk
  through the darkest valley,
I will fear no evil,
  for you are with me;
your rod and your staff,
  they comfort me.

Dark valleys are to happen inevitably because in order to move from place A to place B, we must enter the unknown and that can create anxiety or be scary at times. But there is literally no way around it. The degree of darkness may differ from one journey to the next, but nonetheless, it will exist.

The journey begins by going from learning a new subject, to trying new food, to going from childhood to becoming an adult, to entering a relationship, starting a new job, joining a new team, going through a divorce, raising a child, attending a funeral of a loved one, moving locations, overcoming addictions, inventing a new gadget, starting a business, being promoted to a new position, etc.

We can make the journey more pleasant the more we trust God. We need to remember that there are two journey paths we can take. The journey we created, or the one God creates. When we choose the journey we created, we find ourselves trying to pray God into it, usually to fix it. At times, this journey could align with God's will, but many times, it doesn't so we begin to feel God's silence. Then we increase the intensity of our prayers, hoping to awaken Him for He must be asleep or distracted.

Henry Blackaby, author of the book, *Experiencing God*, states common phrases differently, which I found to be profound. "The typical saying, we use is, 'Just don't stand there do something.' He claims in our interaction with God, that God prefers the statement to read, "Just don't do something, stand there!"

He references the fact that we are to be still enough to listen to God's plan and then join Him on His journey not try to pray God into ours. The formula is not more intense prayer but more stillness in our prayer that we may be guided by God's whisper.

Will Gods plan include peaks and valleys? Absolutely, for we still will enter the unknown. We still will be transformed by His sanctification. We still will be tested and challenged. The difference is we will be following Him who goes ahead of us, who holds our hand, who lifts us up and, at times, carries us so that we can reach his destination for us.

We will find pure joy!

James 1:2-4
Trials and Temptations
2 Consider it pure joy, my brothers and sisters, whenever you face trials of many kinds,³ because you know that the testing of your faith produces perseverance. ⁴ Let perseverance finish its work so that you may be mature and complete, not lacking anything.

When we get to the point of surrender, we too can say with confidence what David proclaimed, "Even when I walk through the darkest of valleys, I will fear no evil for you are with me and your rod and staff shall comfort me."

Think of climbing to the top of Mount Everest with God as your guide, walking along the side of you. The quest will be one of your greatest challenges. The physical and emotional toll will be enormous, including pure anxiety and adrenaline. When you look at the size of the mountain, you tend to scale yourself in relation to it. It's so big and you're so small. Yet, at that moment, God grabs your hand and says, "Let's go" and starts the climb. He looks over at you and sees your uncertainty, anxiousness, and fear. He squeezes your hand, winks at you and says, "Don't worry my child, I was the one who created the mountain, so I know the pathway to the top. Relax and enjoy the journey, I got this!"

Just a Thought…

God's Job is Open,

Applications Being Taken

Position Available: God of the Universe

When filling out your application, please answer the following questions:

What if you were God?
What would you do with all the sickness and disease in the world?
What would you do with all the physical disabilities in the world?
What would you do with all the murderers, rapists, pedophiles, thieves, drug dealers, and child molesters in the world?
What rules, if any, would you set for marriage, infidelity, or sexual orientation?
What laws, if any, would you instill for keeping order in society? If you say no laws, how will you keep order in the world? If you say there are laws, how would they be enforced and what would be the consequence if broken?
What would you do about poverty and wealth?
What would you do with self-centeredness, hatred, lust, selfishness, and greed?
What would you do with the environment, smog, pollution?
What would you do with nature, tsunamis, earthquakes, tornados, hurricanes?
What would say about parenting, work ethic, leadership?
What would you say about money?
What would you say about taxes?
What would you say about war?
Would there be war?
How would you change the way the world and the universe were physically created?
Would you give mankind free will?
What would you say about religions?

How would forgiveness work or would forgiveness even exist?
What would you do with addiction to drugs, alcohol, pornography, co-dependence, food?
What do you do about hunger?
Would there be sadness, depression or loneliness?
How would love be defined?
What emotions would you give to mankind?
Would there be a need for government? If yes, what would the government look like?

Bonus question:

If you started out by saying there is no God, still answer the questions from whatever position you wish. When completed, answer the question what name you would give to how you answered the questions, such as another god, luck, intelligent design, randomness, happenstance, coincidence, etc.

Thank you for applying for the position. As you might imagine, we have had millions of people applying. The people of the world will take your application into consideration and we will get back to you.

Just a Thought…

53
Decision Time

Whom do you fear when faced with a trial in need of deciding to choose?

The world?
What will my friends think?
What will my family think?
How much money it costs?
How will it affect my position?
What will the community think?
What will my boss think?
What will my spouse think?
What will my church think?
What about my ego?
What about my plans I had?
But I really loved him/her.
What about my body?
What about my possessions?
But my heart is broken!
But it's the only one like it.
But what about my business?
But what about my retirement?
Buy what about my security?
But what about my career?
But what about my education?

Abraham was willing to sacrifice his son Isaac, who became the love of his life and by doing so. God said, "Now I know you have chosen me." God stopped Abraham before he was to kill his son. Many times, God just wants us to do a heart check. In Abraham's case, God had very big plans for him, ones that would require Abraham's total allegiance. He needed Abraham to be all in.

On the other hand, when Jesus asked the rich man to give away his resources, the man could not do it and walked away, saddened.

Every time we are faced with the choice to trust God or the world, we make this list.
It then becomes very clear which we will choose. What we don't pay attention to is the condition of our soul, for every time we choose the things of the world, a piece of our soul goes with it. Over time, our soul becomes bankrupt.

The path back to God is narrow but is always the same. It takes only one decision for getting back on course. What is on the list that is in your way today from choosing God?

Just a Thought…

54
Now What?

As I read and learn about the suffering and the journey that one goes through, not only physically and emotionally, but even more so spiritually, I came to the same conclusion. After acknowledging, at all levels, that the journey is overwhelming and torturous at times, we all reach the same question in the end, NOW WHAT?

The doctors deliver the bad news, the family rallies around, the church prays, yet you are left alone to suffer. What do you or can you do? Even God Himself says the suffering may not be taken away.

We understand His teaching on perseverance. We accept that He too has experienced the same pain. Yet again, we are left alone facing the question, NOW WHAT?

Now what am I to do? I'm at the crossroads of life. For at this juncture, there are only two ways to turn. One towards the world and seek relief through the venues it has to offer, or trust that there is a God that can carry you through this suffering in a way that transcends the human understanding. Notice I did not say the suffering will be removed, but rather that He will shore you up during it.

Of course, we all ask for all suffering to be eliminated in the world, yet don't take responsibility for the root reasons it exists in the first place.

So where does that leave us? Back to the question, NOW WHAT?

When left standing facing that juncture, which will you choose? Where will you put your trust? What will be the deciding factor in your decision?

NOW WHAT will you do?

Just a Thought …

55
Approaching God

Ask yourself; "Why am I coming to God? How am I coming to God?"

I am seeking wisdom.
I am seeking discernment.
I am seeking comfort.
I am seeking strength.
I am seeking forgiveness.
I am seeking peace.
I am seeking joy.

The question is for what reason am I seeking these things?
If I were to get all the things I request, then what?
What will I do with all these gifts?

If your answer is you would share them, then you can see why God would want to give them to you. On the other hand, if you keep them to yourself, then you would be out of God's will.

When God asks us to check our motives for prayer, He wants to know what your desire is for asking Him to bless your life.

John 5:19
[19] *Jesus gave them this answer: "Very truly I tell you, the Son can do nothing by himself; he can do only what he sees his Father doing, because whatever the Father does the Son also does.*

Just a Thought…

56
Finally Realized It

When we realize…
When we accept…
When we come to believe…
When the light goes on…
When it finally clicks….

What is behind the word WHEN?
How do we get to that place called WHEN?

WHEN refers to a time in the future that something changes, happens, shifts. What leads up to WHEN and what happens afterward?

Prior to reaching that tipping point, we each go through our own internal analysis of the ideas and/or experiences that surround us. We test, challenge, prod, question until we are comfortable to concede to its reality. The second this happens or "WHEN" it happens, a new word appears: THEN.

THEN refers to a subsequent action that takes place. We do or think or act differently from the prior moment and each moment thereafter.

What happens from that point forward is we tend to question ourselves or forget what brought us to that point of reaching "WHEN", so we revisit the journey repeatedly. But because we have the true experience of living on the other side of WHEN, we can quickly return to where we left off and proceed with life accordingly.

The profound thing with the word WHEN is that it has an endless energy about it. It never stops working, driving us, pushing us to become something more.

WHEN did You realize that?

Just a Thought…

God's Promise

Psalm 46:10
Be still and know that I am God.

Be steadfast, immovable like a statue, in your faith. Know that I will give you wisdom and show you where to go and will guide you and watch over you along the way. You will receive my peace, not the peace that the world talks about, but a peace that transcends all understanding. So, trust in me and my ways with all your heart, mind, and soul and don't lean on your own understanding.

Just watch me and know that it is me working through you and I will set your paths straight. If you get tempted along the way, don't worry, I will provide a way for you to get out. If you get fearful along the way, do not be afraid for my rod and my staff will comfort you. You can be assured that as I was with Moses, I will also be with you, for I will never leave you or forsake you.

Remember that I have a plan for you, not to harm you but to prosper you in accordance with my will for you.

Depend on me and trust me and I will take care of you.

Just a Thought…

58
Surf's Up

Huge waves that would frighten an ordinary swimmer produce a tremendous thrill for the surfer who has ridden them. Let's apply that to our own circumstances. The things we try to avoid and fight against — tribulation, suffering, and persecution — are the very things that produce abundant joy in us.

The underlying foundation of the Christian faith is the undeserved, limitless miracle of the love of God that was exhibited on the Cross of Calvary; a love that is not earned and can never be. Paul said this is the reason that "in all these things we are more than conquerors." We are super-victors with a joy that comes from experiencing the very things which look as if they are going to overwhelm us.

"Oswald Chambers, My Utmost For His Highest".

Why do the waves sometimes feel as if they are new to us, as if we have never experienced them before?

I am sure that there are such things as new waves, bigger and more challenging than before. Yet those familiar waves that keep pounding the shore day after day, shouldn't we face those with extreme confidence? Have we not conquered these many times before? Is it just a matter of not remembering or recognizing the waves? Would it help for us to stop before we enter the waters and take the time to assess the wave? This one I have seen before and this is how God helped me navigate it. Or this one looks a little different, yet it is still a wave made up of the same attributes of the ones in the past. Therefore, I know God delivered me then and He will deliver me now.

Being in the ocean, there are thousands of waves, mostly small but all a little different that keep us on edge and alert always trying to knock us off our board. Yet at certain times of the day or evening, we catch a glimpse when the waters settle down. There is a peacefulness that overtakes us. We can rest. We know that sooner or later the waves will pick back up and we, once again, will be a little stronger this day to battle them.

Then there are those days when we are taken by surprise by a wave that is bigger and stronger and more violent than we have ever experienced. To the novice, the waves will tumble us, yet to the seasoned surfer, it may knock us off the board, but we will draw from past experience and get right back on and ride the wave out. For we know the wave will only last for a short while, then the water will return to it's calm self.

Let us ride the waves of life with the confidence and comfort that God is there with us today as He has been for thousands of waves before.

In the end, it is not the knowledge or understanding that God has the power to rescue us, but it is the love that God has for us that won't allow for Him to not to do so. For God's only weakness, is that He cannot not love us and that love drives Him to do the unimaginable things in our life.

Just a Thought…

59
Going Away Party

John 13:1-5

¹³ It was just before the Passover Festival. Jesus knew that the hour had come for him to leave this world and go to the Father. Having loved his own who were in the world, he loved them to the end.

² The evening meal was in progress, and the devil had already prompted Judas, the son of Simon Iscariot, to betray Jesus. ³ Jesus knew that the Father had put all things under his power, and that he had come from God and was returning to God; ⁴ so he got up from the meal, took off his outer clothing, and wrapped a towel around his waist. ⁵ After that, he poured water into a basin and began to wash his disciples' feet, drying them with the towel that was wrapped around him.

Jesus had something different in mind for His going away party.

Typically, a going away party is designed to honor the guest. To pay tribute, to build up, encourage, affirm, show affection and to reminisce. But Jesus, instead, decided to leave his followers with something different. Instead of them honoring him, he decided to serve them, to show affection towards them, to be humbled before them, to lift them up, and encourage them.

He washed their feet to show how much he loved them, to be an example to them, and to teach them.

He wanted to have a memory that would last and that would serve them well throughout their life.

Instead of them celebrating His leaving, He was giving them the gift.

There was no glory for Him in His miracles. His glory showed up in His overall sacrifice for us. This was what God wanted to convey more than anything else, that we would fully understand how much He loves us and the extent He will go to show us.

Just a Thought…

I Have a Plan for You

Jeremiah 29:11
*¹¹ For I **know** the plans I have for you," declares the Lord, "plans to prosper you and not to harm you, plans to give you hope and a future.*

What does it mean to "know"?

To truly know requires to full and complete understanding of all aspects of the subject at hand. It means that all details have been thought through. It means that you have full understanding and clarity. You know the path to take and the outcome it will bring if followed. It also means that you have control of the outcome.

Jesus says He knows the plans He has for us, so He has given it much concentrated thought down to the minute details. He contemplated every option and weighed them against His unlimited objective, which is to prospers us and to give us hope and a future. Why? Because He cares for us and only wants the best for us. Like a parent, a boss or any person of leadership who sincerely cares for the future of another person, He understands His own heart on this matter and deeply desires that the person in question will trust Him.

It is interesting that Jesus adds a qualifier phrase in this verse, "not to harm you". Why did He feel the necessity to do so?

When another person asks you to follow them, there must be this qualifier in there as it begs the question of trust. The person offering guidance understands the follower's dilemma, the internal question being mulled over. Is this person trustworthy? Is their advice going to have pain in its journey? What am I giving up following what they are saying? The main deciding factor is to give yourself into the hands of another person. TRUST is where we get hung up. A thousand thoughts circle around this single word as we contemplate to move forward or not towards the person's outstretched hand.

This verse requires an action step to be taken. It cannot be read without deciding for yourself if it's true or not and what those implications can mean in your life. You may find yourself skimming over it, but as you go through life, you will always be brought back to this single verse and once again, time after time, be asked to decide the trustworthiness of the author.

What will you do?

Just a Thought…

61
Is Love Enough?

Romans 8:38-39
[38] For I am convinced that neither death nor life, neither angels nor demons, neither the present nor the future, nor any powers, [39] neither height nor depth, nor anything else in all creation, will be able to separate us from the love of God that is in Christ Jesus our Lord.

How much comfort is love amid trials and suffering?
What is it that you seek in times of need?
If you are facing deep physical or emotional pain yet you know you are unconditionally loved by the creator of the universe; will that bring relief?
The question is, how do you perceive love and the love that comes with it?
Is it possible to truly love a person and not provide for them?
Where is the line drawn when people call for tough love?
Does the issue lie with the giver or receiver of love?
Is tough love only needed to drive a person to humility?
Is pure love only found in humility?

Imagine for yourself that you are at a point of great need and you seek God with all your heart, mind, soul, and strength, and He answers you by saying, "Dear one, I want you to know that nothing will separate my love for you." And that's it. Nothing more!

How are you feeling at that moment?
Are you at peace or are you wanting of something more?
Are you thinking love is great, but right now I need help?

Remember you are with God, the almighty creator, healer, comforter.

Can pure love drown out all the feelings of pain and suffering?

There you sit with the arms of our Lord and savior wrapped around you in the most amazing love ever experienced. The circumstance or physical pain has not changed, but for that moment you find that God sized love is bringing you to a place where those things don't seem to matter.

What just happened?
Where did my request for healing or resolution go?

When we strip away expectations out of love, we are left with pure love. Pure love has the ability to bring you to the place where you see God.

Matthew 5:8
[8] Blessed are the pure in heart,
　for they will see God.

Just a Thought …

62
It's No Surprise

When we take time to consider our sinful nature, is it any surprise that trouble or temptation or fear come our way? If that is true, then why do we act so surprised when it does?

Brother Lawrence said that when we begin our spiritual walks, we should take a magnifying glass to ourselves to see what we're made of.

Though we may agree that there is a spiritual battle that surrounds us and that our sinful nature is a result of Satan's schemes, does it really matter where the sin comes from or what is the cause behind it? Or should we just be honest and concede that we have sinned and will continue to sin for that is our nature, and that we, by ourselves, cannot stop doing so on our own? For if we can truly understand this, then, we will understand where sin will lead us eventually. If we survey the events in the world, it is not hard to see the level of depravity that manifests itself when sin is left unchecked.

I think we are surprised when we sin for, we have a false read on ourselves and think we have sin under control. For we will do or think anything other than humbling ourselves by admitting we can't do something and need help from another.

Let us not be surprised by the waves of sin that come our way but rather accept it as fact. We, then, will have the wisdom to prepare ourselves by turning to Christ to give us strength to go about our day. This act will no longer be one of reaction to the surprise of sin but rather a strategic plan to prepare us against it.

We can diminish the fear of sin by replacing it with the power of Christ.

Just a Thought…

63
Mind of Christ

1 Corinthians 2:9-16
⁹ However, as it is written:
"What no eye has seen,
  what no ear has heard,
and what no human mind has conceived" —
  the things God has prepared for those who love him —
¹⁰ these are the things God has revealed to us by his Spirit. The Spirit searches all things, even the deep things of God. ¹¹ For who knows a person's thoughts except their own spirit within them? In the same way no one knows the thoughts of God except the Spirit of God. ¹² What we have received is not the spirit of the world, but the Spirit who is from God, so that we may understand what God has freely given us. ¹³ This is what we speak, not in words taught us by human wisdom but in words taught by the Spirit, explaining spiritual realities with Spirit-taught words. ¹⁴ The person without the Spirit does not accept the things that come from the Spirit of God but considers them foolishness and cannot understand them because they are discerned only through the Spirit. ¹⁵ The person with the Spirit makes judgments about all things, but such a person is not subject to merely human judgments, ¹⁶ for,
"Who has known the mind of the Lord
  so as to instruct him?"
But we have the mind of Christ.

Isn't it true that two people can be standing across from each other, in an intimate relationship, and yet not truly know what the other is thinking? The spirit within each person is personal and only that person is aware of what his or her spirit is thinking or feeling or experiencing.

What would happen if you were able to give your spirit to another person? They would hear your thoughts, experience your emotions. They would know the most intimate you. There would no longer be any secrets about you. They would see into the deepest part of your soul.

Well, maybe it's a good thing we can't do this for each other. Not sure we could bear the vulnerability.

Yet that is exactly what God did. As great as a miracle creation was or the resurrection of Jesus, the fact that God literally gave us His spirit to live inside of us is beyond comprehension. For we now know what God thinks, feels, and His character, His, love, His voice, His heart, His compassion, His wisdom, His discernment are made available to us. All we have to do is submit our spirit to His.

We really do have the MIND of Christ.

What would you do with the mind of Christ today in your work, family and other relationships? Not sure? Stop and submit your spirit to that of Christ and listen. The answer is within you. Ask yourself, "What Would Jesus Think?"

WWJT

Just a Thought…

64
Miracles

Psalms 8:3-4
³ When I consider your heavens,
  the work of your fingers,
the moon and the stars,
  which you have set in place,
⁴ what is mankind that you are mindful of them,
  human beings that you care for them?

Did you know that there are 40 recorded miracles in the New Testament?
   11 miscellaneous
   4 raising from the dead
   25 healings
 There are 56 were recorded in Old Testament
   2 raising from the dead
   1 healing
   53 others
Total
   96 miracles
   6 raising from the dead
   26 healings
   64 others

Oh, did we forget creation? Hmmm. How many miracles are within creation? A million?
The sun
The moon
The stars
The planets
The birds, each individual one
The animals each individual one
Insects, fish
The trees, the flowers, the mountains, the bodies of water,
We can't forget Mankind can we?
The wind
The clouds

The sky
The colors of creation
The reproductive cycle of all things made
Oxygen
Wind, snow, rain

But yet we still, to this day, ask what the disciples asked?

John 6:29-30
[29] Jesus answered, "The work of God is this: to believe in the one he has sent."
[30] So they asked him, "What sign then will you give that we may see it and believe you? What will you do?

What is it today you are asking God to do in order that you will believe in Him?

I dare you to believe.

Just a Thought…

65
Moment by Moment

In that very moment, I ask what choice I have. The moment is coming whether I like it or not.
I have many choices in every moment. If I don't choose, the moment will choose for me.

If I wait to choose, then the moments continue to accumulate and reinforce the one before it.
I can break the chain of moments by choosing a different direction anytime.
It's up to me to determine how long I want to stay in the pattern of the moment.
I choose to trust God in every moment.

I will return to Him and allow Him to guide every moment.
He will provide what I need for the moment and the next one after that and the next.

Just a Thought…

66
Prophet vs Savior

John 6:14
14 After the people saw the sign Jesus performed, they began to say, "Surely this is the Prophet who is to come into the world."

After all the miracles Jesus performed prior to His resurrection, the best they could call Him was a prophet? The difference between prophet and a savior are as wide as the Grand Canyon.

A prophet is someone who foretells about someone or something else. Although profound in nature, there is no personal connection to the prophet. He may amaze people by his skill but nothing more. For it is who or what the prophet is foretelling that has the power to produce the outcome.

A savior, on the other hand, is personal. It's an internal acceptance and submission to the individual.

Therefore Jesus could have performed another thousand miracles and it would have had no effect on the ending.

To accept Jesus as savior puts an end to his need to perform in order to believe. We go from not believing to believing, then to help me with my unbelief.

Satan's job is two-fold:

The first is to keep people at the stage of calling Jesus a prophet for, at best, there is no risk in this. The second job is to convince those who do believe in Jesus as savior that they were wrong in their decision.

So, this is why we pray Lord help me overcome doubt and fear.

You notice now we have gone from asking a prophet to tell us about what is to come, to a personal prayer to help us overcome.

Just a Thought...

Run to Him

Will we run to Him or away from Him?

1 Corinthians 1:21
²¹ For since in the wisdom of God the world through its wisdom did not know him, God was pleased through the foolishness of what was preached to save those who believe.

As we increase in wisdom, one would think we would draw nearer to God. Yet it seems that just the opposite happens. The more wisdom and insight and intelligence we get, the more we boast of ourselves and the more independent we become.

Ask yourself, with each new technological achievement, do we draw closer to God or away from him? Do cell phones draw us closer? Do computers, smart TVs, the Internet, email, video, texting, GPS, robotics, genome study, do they draw us closer to God?

I was watching a show on the genome study, the mapping of DNA, and how they have been able to quantify in the billions of codes, the make-up of a human. Although I walked away in awe of God due to the complexity of our being, I could not help but think, "Will this new intelligence draw us closer or are we on a pursuit to do anything we can to become independent of God?"

Imagine if God unlocked the mysteries of His works. Would we need Him anymore?

I feel we will do anything we can not to have to die to ourselves and avoid submission at all costs.

We are seeking, reading, researching, inventing ways that, hopefully, we can have eternal life on our own terms. Why do we strive so hard to earn it or perform for it, rather than humble ourselves and just receive it?

1 Corinthians 1:25
²⁵ For the foolishness of God is wiser than human wisdom, and the weakness of God is stronger than human strength.

1 Corinthians 1:27-29
²⁷ But God chose the foolish things of the world to shame the wise; God chose the weak things of the world to shame the strong. ²⁸ God chose the lowly things of this world and the despised things—and the things that are not—to nullify the things that are, ²⁹ so that no one may boast before him.

As you stand in wonder of the amazing new things this world can produce, will you run towards God or away from Him? Will you give Him the Glory, or will you give it to man?

Just a Thought…

68
Temptation List

The List

1 Corinthians 10:13
¹³ No temptation has overtaken you except what is common to mankind. And God is faithful; he will not let you be tempted beyond what you can bear. But when you are tempted, he will also provide a way out so that you can endure it.

Temptations, (Satan's weapons)

- Pride
- Lust
- Greed
- Fear
- Doubt
- Coveting
- Money
- Food
- Power
- Affirmation
- Anger
- Myself
- Gossip
- Scarcity
- Hurry
- Busyness

When I wake, I walk into a world that is filled with the list of temptations. These are available 24/7, 365 days a year. The lie is that I must choose one, as if there is not another list to pick from. So I go about my day fending off the temptations as I seek God's strength.

But what if there is another list that looks like this?

- Love
- Joy
- Peace
- Patience
- Kindness
- Self-control
- Grace
- Mercy
- Forgiveness
- Serving
- Generosity
- Purity
- Simplicity
- Gratefulness
- Confidence
- Trust
- Contentment
- Abundance
- Others

If I choose to pick from this list, then I will go about my day seeking God's strength to engage in my choice. The funny thing is, this list is also available 24/7, 365 days a year.

Which will you choose?

Just a Thought…

69
Work to Do

John 6:27-29
²⁷ Do not work for food that spoils, but for food that endures to eternal life, which the Son of Man will give you. For on him God the Father has placed his seal of approval."
²⁸ Then they asked him, "What must we do to do the works God requires?"
²⁹ Jesus answered, "The work of God is this: to believe in the one he has sent."

John 6:60
⁶⁰ On hearing it, many of his disciples said, "This is a hard teaching. Who can accept it?"

John 6:66
⁶⁶ From this time many of his disciples turned back and no longer followed him.

What work are we to do? We are to believe.

Why is this so hard, so much so that many disciples turned away from Jesus and stopped following him? What is it about belief in something that is so hard? What happens when we believe?
We become exposed, vulnerable, at risk. We transfer trust from ourselves onto something or someone else. Belief is giving up ourselves, our pride, our ego, our things, our trust, our position, our money, our soul to another.

Have you ever considered the fact that the closer it gets to the heart the harder it becomes? For example, we believe in thousands of things every day without giving it much thought. The sun coming up, the car that we get in, the planes we fly on, the air we breathe. Yet, we have no emotional attachment. Now consider what it takes to believe in the doctor who is diagnosing your cancer, the girlfriend who says she did not cheat on you, the boss who is controlling your future, or the friend you are confiding in.

You can see how the level of difficulty increases the more personal it becomes.

So, now Jesus asks you to give up all your beliefs and entrust Him with them. Trust Him for food, clothing, shelter, money, career, relationships, health, your future.

Wow! What a big ask from Jesus.

Will you stay, or will you leave? Are His teachings too hard?

Just a Thought…

70
From Wailing to Dancing

Exodus 14:10
[10] As Pharaoh approached, the Israelites looked up, and there were the Egyptians, marching after them. They were terrified and cried out to the Lord.

... The Journey In Between ...
Exodus 15:20-21
[20] Then Miriam the prophet, Aaron's sister, took a timbrel in her hand, and all the women followed her, with timbrel and dancing. [21] Miriam sang to them:
"Sing to the Lord,
  for he is highly exalted.
Both horse and driver
  he has hurled into the sea."

It took just one chapter, but they had to go through the Red Sea to experience it.

We, too, go through chapters in life. Some chapters are short and some are long, but eventually you get to the next chapter.

Your chapter in life could be four years of school, nine month of pregnancy, two years of engagement, ten years of an illness, two weeks of a vacation, twenty-four hours of waiting for that call. Each one builds on the prior one as the story unfolds.

Like a book, you can read the beginning and the end but you will never know the story without reading all the chapters.

Our lives have a beginning and an end, but our story is the journey in the middle.

Consider looking at your current chapter — or your circumstances — as temporary but knowing patiently that it has to be written before moving to the next one.

Just a Thought...

Walking through a Miracle

Exodus 14:21-22
21 Then Moses stretched out his hand over the sea, and all that night the Lord drove the sea back with a strong east wind and turned it into dry land. The waters were divided, 22 and the Israelites went through the sea on dry ground, with a wall of water on their right and on their left.

What were the people thinking as they walked through the parted sea?
Some were very anxious and bewildered and walked with trepidation.
Some walked with amazement and awe.
Some walked trying to figure out the engineering of the whole feat.
Some walked with doubt until they reached the other side.
Some walked in laughter out of pure joy.
Some walked to total peace always knowing that God was with them.
Some walked with great confidence and boldness.
Some trusted at the first step, some trust came as each step they took, and some trust only came when they reached the other side and looked back.

When we see God performing miracles in and around us, how do we walk through them?

Just a Thought…

72
A Glimpse of Beauty in the Darkness

Imagine you are in a desert and have been there for days without water. You begin to lose hope. Your mind is conceding to the negative thoughts that are bombarding you – when in the distance, you see a body of water. Your heart races. The negative thoughts are replaced with ones of anticipation.

Water never looked so good, and you imagine all the great images you can conjure up about refreshing water: The taste of it going down as you take a drink, the refreshing feel of it on your body when you shower, the fun you experienced when you would play in it. Water was never so beautiful as it is this very moment, during your trial in the desert.

This is how Jesus looks when we are in our deepest and darkest moments. He is never more beautiful. When we lose all hope and give in to despair, there, in the distance, we see Jesus with a smile on His face, compassion in His eyes. His arms stretched out toward us. We see His magnificent power and glory and as we move forward toward Him, the darkness gets left behind. We rejoice once again in our savior.

[17] *Though the fig tree does not bud*
 and there are no grapes on the vines,
though the olive crop fails
 and the fields produce no food,
though there are no sheep in the pen
 and no cattle in the stalls,
[18] *yet I will rejoice in the Lord,*
 I will be joyful in God my Savior.

Just a Thought…

73
What is God Thinking?

We are asked by God that our thoughts be His thoughts, but what is God thinking? I believe God's thoughts are something like this:

Do not worry about tomorrow as today will have enough trials, and who, by worrying, can change anything?
Do not be anxious about anything, I will give you peace.
Seek me first and all else will be given to you.
Don't worry about temptations as I will give you a way out.
Love your spouse.
Love your children.
Love your friend that you would give your life for them.
Love your neighbor as you love yourself.
Work with excellence at your job.
You can do anything you try when you seek my help.
Pick today: money or me — you can't serve both.
Take care of the widows, orphans, the poor, and the oppressed.
Lead by serving.
Don't rush to be first.
Be patient and kind.
Be still at times throughout the day so you can hear me.
Be joyful to the fullest.
Don't be afraid of anything or anyone.
Go the extra mile when helping someone.
When you get tired and weary, come to me and I will revitalize you. I'll even carry you if needed.
You will never be alone for I will never leave you or forget about you.
Comfort those who need comfort, just as I have comforted you.
Stare into the heavens and be amazed at my creation.
Enjoy this day as it is one of my creations.

Are these your thoughts today?

Just a Thought... or should I say, just God's Thoughts?

74
God is Beautiful

During my quiet time this morning, I reflected on ACTS, an acronym for Adoration, Confession, Thanksgiving, Supplication.

In thinking about how I adore God, I said, *"God is beautiful."* That got me thinking about how he is beautiful and began to list the ways.

His creation is amazingly beautiful, from the sunrise to the sunset, from mountains to the vast seas, from the spider to the whale, from blue to all the colors in the rainbow, from a flower to the oak tree. His creation of mankind is beautiful, and that got me thinking about how beautiful it is when a person is doing what is right.

They will feel healthy when they take care of their bodies.
They will feel creative when they slow down and observe their surroundings.
They will feel compassion toward others when they give, and their hearts will melt.
They will feel strong when they stand up for what is right.
They will feel loved when they show love.
They will feel embraced by a holy God when they worship Him.
They will feel peace when they follow His ways.
They will not be anxious about anything when they are still before God.
They will live in great expectation for each day filled with a joy.
They will make great friends when they give of themselves.
They will feel affirmed by God when they serve others.
They will not feel worry when they learn to trust God.
They will always have enough when they find God to be sufficient.
They will not experience fear but rather peace, courage, and strength when they let God be their source.
They will have wisdom and discernment when they seek God's advice.
They will find laughter, pure joy, excitement, fun, and happiness in the ways of God.

They will find passion as they are used by God.

This life is available to us every single day — including today, right now!

We don't have to wait until we are in heaven to experience life in this way. It can be heaven on earth if we just decide to do things God's way.

Just a Thought...

75
The Magic Moment

"God never made salvation dependent upon new moons or holy days or Sabbaths. A man is not nearer to Christ on Easter Sunday than he is, say, on Saturday, August 3, or Monday, October 4. As long as Christ sits on the mediatorial throne, every day is a good day and all days are days of salvation." – The Pursuit of God, AW Tozer

When do you find yourself closest to God? Is it a time of day, a certain place or maybe a holiday or a season or when you are with a certain person or sitting in church? Can you tell when you feel close to Him? Can you explain it to someone else what you experience when it happens?

I used to feel close to God when I was emotionally in a good place. The better I felt, the more I felt His presence. Logic would support this. Then one day in 1997, while on a train to Chicago, God explained to me that faith is not an emotion, it is a fact. No matter how I was feeling or what circumstances I was facing, it had nothing to do with who God was.

Hebrews 11:1
11 Now faith is confidence in what we hope for and assurance about what we do not see.

At first, I was disappointed to find this out. I liked the feeling of being close to God. It was a good emotional experience. However, the more I began to think about it, the clearer it became. By using emotion, or time of day or season of the year or any other means to feel closer to God, the more it meant that I was determining how the relationship was going to go and I was governing God's power by my limitations. The better my emotions or environment were, the more powerful God appeared to be.

Yet when I remove myself from the control seat, put my faith in the facts of who God is, a transforming power of God begins within me. As I read scripture, my heart is encouraged, comforted, separated from my emotions or surroundings. His word takes control of my life. In the midst of a chaotic world, I can find peace. In the depths of uncertainty, I am planted on solid ground. In the darkest moments, I can see light.

I began to feel the freedom of knowing that God's greatness had nothing to do with me. He was, is and always will be great in every minute of every day of every year, in good times and in bad, in struggles and in peace, in wealth and in poverty. God is God.

What does this mean for us? It means that 24/7, 365 days a year, we can be close to God. We can experience God the same way on Christmas as we do on Saturday doing chores. Don't believe me? Stop what you're doing this very moment. Reach for your bible or get on your knees, or simply close your eyes and begin to seek Him wholeheartedly. He will take you beyond your emotional capacity and transform your heart, mind, and soul. The world around you will shrink in size. Elections, World Series, the economy, ISIS, or protests in the streets will all fade away.

Need some help? Try reading this psalm over and over again and see if Christmas doesn't show up today!

Psalm 23
A psalm of David.
1 The Lord is my shepherd, I lack nothing.
2   He makes me lie down in green pastures,
he leads me beside quiet waters,
3   he refreshes my soul.
He guides me along the right paths
*   for his name's sake.*
4 Even though I walk
*   through the darkest valley,*
I will fear no evil,
*   for you are with me;*
your rod and your staff,
*   they comfort me.*
5 You prepare a table before me
*   in the presence of my enemies.*
You anoint my head with oil;
*   my cup overflows.*

⁶ *Surely your goodness and love will follow me*
  all the days of my life,
and I will dwell in the house of the Lord
  forever.

Just a Thought…

76
Moving Forward

Have you ever tried to stop moving forward? Is it even possible? In business the saying goes that you're either moving forward or moving backward — there is no middle ground. Or, as the other saying goes, "Stop and think about it!"

But can we stop? I would argue we cannot stop. The mere fact that time doesn't stop or go in reverse leaves me to believe we are always moving forward . This is a fact beyond our control.

If that's true, what does that mean? If moving forward is inevitable, then each second that passes is a new second to be experienced in a new way.

"It is not so much adverse events that make you anxious as it is your thoughts about those events. Your mind engages in efforts to take control of a situation, to bring about the result you desire. Your thoughts close in on the problem like ravenous wolves. Determined to make things go your way, you forget that I am in charge of your life. The only remedy is to switch your focus from the problem to my presence.

"When things don't go as you would like, accept the situation immediately. If you indulge in feelings of regret, they can easily spill
  Sarah Young's Jesus Calling: Enjoying Peace in His Presence
over the line into resentment."

As Sarah Young says, each new moment gives you the ability to change what happened the moment prior. If we accept each moment in the moment — as just a moment, without adding anything to it — it's not the circumstance, it's the thought about the circumstance that causes our reaction and we can experience something new.

If God says He is with us and will guide us, then we must believe that this is true in every moment.

At any moment in time we can change the direction of our thoughts, never looking back at the prior moment in regret, for that moment is gone, but looking forward, striving to keep our focus on our Lord and savior, Jesus.

"The ultimate challenge is to keep fixing your eyes on me, no matter what is going on around you. When I am central in your thinking, you are able to view circumstances from my perspective."
Sarah Young's *Jesus Calling: Enjoying Peace in His Presence*
 over the line into resentment."

Now just take a moment to think about this.

Just a Thought…

How to Stay Clear of God

"How shall we do this?" his demons shouted. "Keep them busy in the non-essentials of life and invent innumerable schemes to occupy their minds," he answered.

"Tempt them to spend, spend, spend, and borrow, borrow, borrow."

"Persuade the wives to go to work for long hours and the husbands to work 6-7 days each week, 10-12 hours a day, so they can afford their empty lifestyles."

"Keep them from spending time with their children."

"As their family's fragment, soon, their homes will offer no escape from the pressures of work!"

"Over-stimulate their minds so that they cannot hear that still, small voice."

"Entice them to play the radio or iPod whenever they drive and keep the TV, DVDs, CDs and their PCs going constantly in their homes and see to it that every store and restaurant in the world plays non-biblical music constantly."

"This will jam their minds and break that union with CHRIST."

"Fill the coffee tables with magazines and newspapers."

"Pound their minds with the news 24 hours a day."

"Invade their driving moments with billboards."

"Flood their mailboxes with junk mail, mail order catalogs, sweepstakes, and every kind of newsletter, and promotional offering free products, services, and false hopes."

"Keep skinny, beautiful models on the magazines and TV so their husbands will believe that outward beauty is what's important and they'll become dissatisfied with their wives."

"Keep the wives too tired to love their husbands at night."

"Give them headaches too!"

"If they don't give their husbands the love they need, they will begin to look elsewhere."

"That will fragment their families quickly!"

"Give them Santa Claus to distract them from teaching their children the real meaning of Christmas."

"Give them an Easter bunny so they won't talk about His resurrection and power over sin and death…"

"Even in their recreation, let them be excessive."
"Have them return from their recreation exhausted."

"Keep them too busy to go out in nature and reflect on GOD'S creation. Send them to amusement parks, sporting events, plays, concerts, and movies instead."

"Keep them busy, busy, busy!"

"And when they meet for spiritual fellowship, involve them in gossip and small talk so that they leave with troubled consciences."

"Crowd their lives with so many good causes they have no time to seek power from JESUS."

"Soon they will be working in their own strength, sacrificing their health and family for the good of the cause."

"It will work!"

"It will work!"

It was quite a plan!

The demons went eagerly to their assignments causing Christians everywhere to get busier and more rushed, going here and there, having little time for their GOD or their families. Having no time to tell others about the power of JESUS to change lives.

I guess the question is, has the devil been successful in his schemes?

You be the judge!

Does "BUSY" mean: B-eing U-nder S-atan's Y-oke?

Please pass this on, if you aren't too BUSY!

Do you love Him?

IF YOU LOVE JESUS, PASS THIS ON!!!

Just A Thought…

78
In the Moment

Luke 12:25
25 Who of you by worrying can add a single hour to your life?

What would it be like to just live in the moment?

It sounds nice and is portrayed as being something good. I understand this perspective when I consider everything outside the moment as creating regret, worry, anxiety, stress or fear. But what about when the actual moment is all these things? Imagine if in the moment, you are being tortured or harmed or injured or received bad news? Don't you want to be anywhere else but "in the moment"?

Is there something even more immediate, more conscious, than the moment that could elevate us out of it, even the most difficult times?

What was Jesus focused on in his moments of being flogged, ripped apart, mocked, spit on? Where was he mentally?

Are moments broken down to split seconds? Was Jesus in between each moment of the whip slashing across his back, in total focus on God?

The Bible talks about people like Stephen being stoned to death or Daniel in the lions' den. God can meet us in the exact seconds of each moment to help us endure the most trying and painful of times.

Isn't it in those exact single seconds of time when we decide if God is real? Don't we cry out to Him?

For someone outside the faith — as well as those who are seasoned veterans — these moments can be defining moments in your relationship with God. Just like Brother Lawrence, the more you practice you have with being present with God, the readier you will be for the next moment!

When you string enough moments together where you are present with God, it becomes a state of peaceful being. There's no looking forward or back — you're just being in the moment.

Just a Thought…

79
When Do We Let God Off the Hook?

Deuteronomy 31: 6
⁶ Be strong and courageous. Do not be afraid or terrified because of them, for the Lord your God goes with you; he will never leave you nor forsake you."

What a great victory statement Moses wrote here. Can you feel the power in his words?

Have you ever been victorious in something that has been extremely difficult? Maybe you are at that point right now but just haven't stopped long enough to look back on where you came from and what it took to get where you are today.

I am reminded of a single mom who gets up every morning to care for her children sacrificing all she has inside her to persevere throughout the day, every day. There are very few moments she can slow down to see how she can say the words that Paul said. She has struggled but has not been defeated.

I can think of so many people who have been victorious over job loss, financial ruin, medical problems, depression, addiction, abandonment, divorce, loss of a child or loved one, handicaps, acts of racism, poverty, and religious persecution. Yet as I read the scripture again, the question came. When do we let God off the hook? When do we finally concede that God is for us and He will carry us through the most difficult times in our life? When do we acknowledge His unwavering faithfulness? When do we become in awe of His power, His compassion, His grace?

It has been a pattern of mankind from the beginning of time to struggle, for God to deliver us from struggle. For us to praise God but then to lose sight of Him until the next struggle comes, only then to question as to where He is or why this or that is happening or how am I going to survive. Can we ever reach a point that we face each new trial with confidence and not ask God to have to prove Himself over and over again, but rather to now know for absolute certainty what He means when He says He will never leave us or forsake us and that he will give us strength to do all things through Him and to ultimately treat all trials past, present, and future with pure joy?

James 1:2-4
Trials and Temptations
[2] Consider it pure joy, my brothers and sisters, whenever you face trials of many kinds, [3] because you know that the testing of your faith produces perseverance. [4] Let perseverance finish its work so that you may be mature and complete, not lacking anything.

Stop today for a moment and assess your life and take inventory of how God has been there for you and conclude for yourself that He is truly God. And then take your next step boldly and with a smile as you recite your victory verse He has written on your heart.

If you have not experienced God in such a way to praise Him for your trials, then I encourage you to draw closer to Him and you too will have the chance to experience how a great God can work in your life.

Luke 12: 22 –26
Do Not Worry
[22] Then Jesus said to his disciples: "Therefore I tell you, do not worry about your life, what you will eat; or about your body, what you will wear. [23] For life is more than food, and the body more than clothes. [24] Consider the ravens: They do not sow or reap, they have no storeroom or barn; yet God feeds them. And how much more valuable you are than birds! [25] Who of you by worrying can add a single hour to your life? [26] Since you cannot do this very little thing, why do you worry about the rest?

See you in the victor's circle!

Just a Thought…

80
Fix your Eyes Upon Jesus

Psalms 141:8
⁸ But my eyes are fixed on you, Sovereign Lord;
  in you I take refuge—do not give me over to death.

Fix your eyes upon Jesus. How do you do that? When you fix your eyes upon something, you stare, focus, gaze, concentrate on a physical thing. So how do I fix my eyes on Jesus in this world?

I see things as Jesus does: creation as being amazing, people as being miraculous, animals as being outrageous signs of creativity.
I see people in need of a Savior.
I see the church as the hope of the world.
I see the beauty of sunsets and flowers.
I see friends, family, jobs, food, clothing and shelter as gifts.
I see opportunities to serve others.
I see the tasks before me as small and not threatening as I filter them through the power of Christ.
I no longer fear going out into the world but go with anticipation and excitement. I go knowing Jesus goes with me.

How cool is that to have the Almighty God walking ahead and beside you?

Consider if you were walking with a famous person — people might look your way with envy. Well, to be walking with Almighty God at your side, the all-powerful, the all-loving, the all-knowing, the almighty. How big would the strut in your step be? How wide your smile? How peaceful your heart?

Where will you fix your eyes today?

What will you see?

Just a Thought...

81
What Can I Bring?

What do I bring into this day?

In the story of Abraham being asked to sacrifice his son Isaac, we must ask why did that have to happen? Was that some cruel, diabolical plan of a deranged God? God, after 100 years, gives Abraham a son he has asked for only to tell him he now needs to sacrifice him? Or was this Abraham's doing? How can it be Abraham's doing one might ask? You first must ask what God was trying to accomplish by such a harsh test.

What is God after in all of us? God's only desire from us is that we give Him our heart. Whatever competes in our heart against God, He will seek to remove. In the story, Abraham replaced God with Isaac. Abraham began worshiping the gift rather than the giver. Prior to the birth of Isaac, Abraham was dependent on God. However, after receiving Isaac, Abraham, though very grateful for Isaac, began focusing his attention on his son and away from God. What's the big deal?

God had great plans for Abraham. He was going to build an entire nation under him, as many as the stars in the sky or particles of sand on a sea shore. God has said from the very beginning, that we are to have no other gods before Him. God knew what He had to do to restore Abraham's heart back into a right relationship with him. So the question stands. Why such a harsh test?

I propose that Abraham brought this upon himself the minute he replaced God with Isaac. We ask God to be the center of our life, or we sing, "my soul's desire is to worship you". Then God is left with no other choice but to perform surgery and remove that which is attached to our hearts that has replaced God. When we talk about heart surgery, it is a very intricate and painful process.

God has always provided the things in life we require and would want. From creation, whereby everything created was for our benefit and His glory, to creating mankind and companionship to meet our emotional and physical needs. But God never intended that any of those things were to replace Him on the throne of our worship.

Can we avoid trials such as Abraham's? Yes, if we seek to empty ourselves of anything that has taken up even the smallest residency of our heart. If our heart is pure, then there would be no need for surgery now, would there? On the other hand, the more we become attached to that which has attached itself to our hearts, the more severe the surgery will have to be.

What can I bring each day to God? Nothing. It's more of what can I leave behind.

Just a Thought…

82
He had Everything but He Possessed Nothing

"He had everything, but he possessed nothing." – The Pursuit of God, AW Tozer

This phrase was referring to Abraham after he was tested to sacrifice his son Isaac. This statement is deeply profound if, when you read it, you allow God to speak to you.

Spend a few minutes with God and see what He says about it. Here is what I heard Him say. Make a list of everything you have. I did this briefly and listed my wife, family, friends, church, clothes, food, technology, money, church, transportation, toys, home, job, and more. Then He asked me who owns these things? Possess means to own. If you truly own something, it can't be taken away from you. What did I really own? All the things I listed are things that I have but they could be taken from me at any time.

I was left possessing nothing but having everything. At first a sadness appeared, then a joy followed as I realized I was free from the stress that comes from protecting, hoarding, or being overly emotionally attached to these things I thought I owned. When we own things, they not only take up a part of our physical ability to manage, but also our emotional being as well. We don't even realize that we are connected so tightly until something we own is gone.

God showed Abraham this by asking him to sacrifice his son.

God is not saying we can't love, care for, or even enjoy, the things or people we have in our lives, but we need to recognize that we own nothing. All we have is God's. We are to be His stewards.

What I found the minute I understood the difference between owning and having, was relief, joy, and peace. For a brief moment, I felt my heart was totally emptied and room for more of God was made available. Changing my thinking is also changing my seeing. I am now starting to look at my list of things I thought I owned differently.

Do you see the slight differences? When you don't own something, the responsibility shifts from you to the real owner, God. My car, for example. I now see I have it but don't own it. I will be a good steward and take care of it, but should it go away it is now up to God to replace it as He deems to do so. He knows my need for transportation, so I can trust that He will indeed replace it or provide other means.

So, what are we to do with this newfound freedom? We can use this time to draw near to God. By doing so we will be free to be used by Him. The things we have are now available as well to be used for His glory.

One test you can take to see how you are faring in understanding this profound thinking is this. Take something from the list you made and give it away. The harder it is to give away will show you how much you think you own it.

Just a Thought…

83
Looking in All the Wrong Places

Matthew 10:39
³⁹ Whoever finds their life will lose it, and whoever loses their life for my sake will find it.

Have you ever stopped and asked yourself, what am I looking for out of this life? Each morning as you think about the day ahead, what is it you hope for? Have you ever given something away that was of importance to you only to walk away feeling extremely joyful? Have you served, or been compassionate, or cared for another person even when you didn't want to? Have you ever achieved or experienced something great beyond your dreams only to find after the celebration, you were left with still yearning for more out of life?

Jesus talks about a radical experience when He says when we lose our life on behalf of Him that we will find what we are looking for. What are we looking for? Why do we strive so hard for something that will produce no return on our investment?

God says when we seek Him, we will find him and when we give ourselves to Him, we will receive life itself. When we receive life from God, we receive the fruits of the spirit the same way fruit is the offspring of an apple tree.

Galatians 5:22-23
²² But the fruit of the Spirit is love, joy, peace, forbearance, kindness, goodness, faithfulness,²³ gentleness and self-control. Against such things there is no law.

As we go about our day, we must ask ourselves again, what do I want to look for in my day; the things the world has told me or those that God has made available?

Oh, I almost forgot, there is a catch. When you seek the things of the world, that's all you get. When you seek the ways of God, He has a way of throwing in the good things of the world as a bonus!

You will be looking for something today, just try not to look in all the wrong places.

Just a Thought…

84
Peace

Philippians 4:6-7
⁶ Do not be anxious about anything, but in every situation, by prayer and petition, with thanksgiving, present your requests to God. ⁷ And the peace of God, which transcends all understanding, will guard your hearts and your minds in Christ Jesus.

God could have chosen anything to protect our hearts; why peace? He could have chosen joy, confidence, courage, wisdom, love, power — but why peace?

Can you remember the last time you experienced true peace? First, peace is the only antidote for anxiety. Anxiety takes a toll on your body and mind. It creates a mental state of confusion, insecurity, anger, resentment, frustration, poor judgement, exhaustion, and isolation. The physical body will become weak, fatigued, sickly, with an increased heart rate, sleeplessness, muscle tension, inadequate blood flow, and shortness of breath.

But one simple word — peace — can change all that.

That word must be supported by a large supply of ingredients to wipe out all those symptoms of anxiety. Are there different types of peace? God says we will receive His peace and His peace transcends all understanding.

There are a lot of ways to experience at least some kind of peace: meditating, or just sitting and gazing at a sunrise or sunset, or sitting in a recliner listen to relaxing music, or on a deck just taking in nature. These are ways to take an educated inventory of what exactly is going on with your mind and body. But this peace that God says we will get is beyond our understanding.

I have experienced this peace. I can only describe it as a sense of the accumulation of all the combined ingredients of joy, strength, wisdom, courage, power, love, trust, patience and comfort — and not knowing where or how it's happening to you.

It's a feeling like a blanket being wrapped around you when you are chilled, or an arm on your shoulder when you are sad, or a chair put under you when you are weak, or a glass of water when you are thirsty. It encompasses all your body, mind and soul. The weight of the world is lifted and scaled down to a simple size.

Then the greatest secret ingredient kicks in: You automatically begin to love others. Compassion, understanding, forgiveness, and encouragement for others, kicks in. You become moved to action. The sense of the things that caused the initial anxiety is gone and the gift of anticipation, and excitement starts to take over. A frown turns to a smile. Teary eyes become wide with sparkle and the heart starts to pump again with blood flowing to all parts of the body, energizing each part.

And then you acknowledge God, for you know at the deepest part of your soul that this was a gift and not of your own doing.

Just a Thought…

85
Do You Really Know Me?

"And this is life eternal, that they might know thee, the only true God and Jesus Christ, whom thou hast sent." – The Pursuit of God, AW Tozer

If you have been married for 50 years, do you know everything about your spouse? Have you stopped trying to get to know them better? Has your curiosity or a sincere interest been satisfied? Could this be the root of boredom or lack of intimacy in the relationship? Does this hold true for a parent towards their child or between two best friends? Do we have internal limits where we decide we are done learning more about the other person?

I would guess unless the other person caught us by their surprise action or response, that we are good for now with what we know of them. By doing this, we have put them in a box never to come out. Yet, we have seen when a relationship falls apart and a new relationship forms with another person, we observe new dimensions expressing themselves. The best we can say is, "Wow, I didn't know that he or she could do that or was even interested in that!" Is it possible that we have done the same with God?

Have we hit our limit of knowing Him? Have we stopped trying to know Him? Unless God does something to surprise us, have we become bored with God?

I see how this can easily happen. When we seek God to meet our needs, we can set a limit on how we experience God. Yet, on the other hand, if we seek to join God in His ways, then we will be taken on a limitless adventure. It is impossible for us to imagine what all the possibilities are?

Life would be exciting, and we would awake with great anticipation toward the day ahead. This has nothing to do with our current trials or pains or sufferings. For they will always be there or, if removed, only to be replaced with new ones. No, this is about seeking God beyond our needs and wants to find out more about His.

The funny thing is God says, "If you seek after me, not only will you find me but while you are pursuing me, I will take those things that you are struggling with from you." If we seek to know more about our spouse, friend or child we will grow deeper in our love for them. When we seek to know God more each and every day, He will amaze us, and our hearts will grow bigger.

Jeremiah 29:12 –13
[12] Then you will call on me and come and pray to me, and I will listen to you. [13] You will seek me and find me when you seek me with all your heart.

Just a Thought…

86
Did God Really Say...?

Genesis 3:1

Did God really say…? That was the million-dollar question. Satan must have contemplated for some time what would he say to his very first encounter with God's newly created person.

Did God really say…
That He is God
That He loves us
That He will protect us
To trust Him
Not to lie
Not to gossip
Not to steal
Not to covet
To be still
To be kind
To be at peace
Not to worry
Not to be anxious
To do good
To hate evil
Not to love money
To give to the poor
To help the widow and orphan
To be strong
To be courageous
There will be troubles, but he overcame these
To be patient
To love your spouse
Not to exasperate your children
To train up ourselves
He will give us joy
To live life fully
He will give us a way out of temptation
We will have eternal life if we believe in Jesus
To speak truth

To guard our minds
He will never leave us
He dwells inside us
To love our enemies
To work as if he was our boss
To give freely
He will provide for us
Not to worship other gods
He forgives us
He is a jealous God
He will come for us
To spread His word
To confess our sins
Not to eat from the tree of knowledge of good and evil
I will give you my peace
I am the way, the truth, the life
Where your heart so is your treasure
I will turn all things for good for those love me
To speak truth in love

If He did really say these things, what does that mean for you?

Just a Thought…

87
Lean on Me

Isaiah 41:13
¹³ For I am the Lord your God
  who takes hold of your right hand
and says to you, Do not fear;
  I will help you.

Proverbs 3:5-6
⁵ Trust in the Lord with all your heart
  and lean not on your own understanding;
⁶ in all your ways submit to him,
  and he will make your paths straight.

Psalm 121:1-2
¹ I lift up my eyes to the mountains—
  where does my help come from?
² My help comes from the Lord,
  the Maker of heaven and earth.

Psalm 23:1-2
A psalm of David.
¹ The Lord is my shepherd, I lack nothing.
²   He makes me lie down in green pastures,
he leads me beside quiet waters,

Isaiah 40:29
²⁹ He gives strength to the weary
  and increases the power of the weak.

Psalm 16:8
⁸ I keep my eyes always on the Lord.
  With him at my right hand, I will not be shaken.

Do you find it interesting that our entire life we seek independence, to learn how to build ourselves up, educate ourselves, and pride ourselves on being independent? We drive cars, wear clothes, sport hairstyles, and tattoos to show we are independent.

Yet, in the end when independence didn't sustain us in our times of trouble, we revert to being dependent on someone or something.

God has this figured out. He wants us to be so dependent on Him that He will give us total independence from the things of this world. He says He will protect us, provide for us, comfort us, love us, give us strength, perseverance, peace and joy. We can live without fear or condemnation. We can have abundance and live life fully. Then, to top it off, He gives us power over death through eternal life with Him!

Ask yourself what person, company, amount of money, power, prestige, medication, addiction, exercise, location, can you depend on in life to provide you all this? All else, besides depending on God, is like building your house on sinking sand.

Why then do we fight off the need to be dependent on something or someone? At the root you will find pride is the culprit.

How does it sound if you admit to those around you that you are dependent upon God for all things in life? If we are honest with ourselves, we would like to say, "I depend on God for certain things but for the most part, I'm in charge for most everything in my life."

God asks for 100% dependence on Him. Is he a control freak or a very wise God? His formula states the more you die to yourself and depend on Him, the freer and more independent you truly are.

Matthew 10:39
39 Whoever finds their life will lose it, and whoever loses their life for my sake will find it.

Try admitting you can't and start agreeing that God can and see where God leads you today.

Just a Thought...

Trust

Trust is defined as the firm belief in the reliability, truth, ability and strength of someone or something. Trust is a simple, five-letter word. Yet behind this word are other words that have years of experience in supporting its meaning.

Reliability, for example. A reliable person will have to have proven themselves to be there on a consistent basis each time you call upon them. When they show up, they are consistent in their actions; you would never question what you would expect from them. You know that one call and they are there for you: never late, always attentive and always with time for you.

Truth. Truth itself must be proven over time. For what is truth but an opinion of how things really are? But today, people choose to believe what is true or not, so for a person's opinion to be found true, there have to be experiences that will support or deny this truth. As these experiences accumulate, they begin to support your belief in what is at hand as being the truth. Truth has to be tested over time and multiple times before it is firmly believed as being absolute truth.

Ability. Ability is an encompassing word. It can be singular in nature, such the ability to do a certain task, or it can be broad in that one can do many tasks. The key is that we associate a level of competency to the word ability for it to have any purposeful meaning. We can say that a person could do that task, but we are at the exact same time filtering that comment by expectations of that person's strength, education, social skills, influence, status, and wealth. For a person to have the ability to do all things, he would need to be proficient in every category. For someone to have a greater ability than all people, he would have to have set the standards himself. Ability must be tested against all its opponents to determine at what level the ability can be accomplished.

Strength. Strength must be tested against opposing forces to be fully assessed. It can be a counterweight to be lifted, a worthy opponent to fend off, a task that takes extreme perseverance, a crisis that takes exceptional fortitude, or restraint to withhold the use of power, emotion and compassion when necessary. Strength is always being tested against time, for time will eventually weaken strength. Time will add or subtract the validity of strength. To be strong for a moment pales against being strong over great lengths of time.

"Do you trust me?" To answer that question, you must reflect on the person's reliability, truth, ability, and strength. For simple matters, trust can be minimized and even risked. For meaningful life questions, trust must be thoroughly assessed. There is, at the center of trusting someone, the moment you exchange a piece of yourself for that of another. You give that part of yourself over to the person to do what they claim they can do.

God says to trust Him with all your heart, mind, and soul. Leaders ask their followers to trust them; to lead them on the journey.

Each day we are faced with hundreds of trust opportunities. Some are very small, and some can alter our lives. No one escapes the question.

Who will you trust today?

Just a Thought…

89
Patience

2 Peter 3:8-9
⁸ But do not forget this one thing, dear friends: With the Lord a day is like a thousand years, and a thousand years are like a day. ⁹ The Lord is not slow in keeping his promise, as some understand slowness. Instead he is patient with you, not wanting anyone to perish, but everyone to come to repentance.

So many times, I think that God needs to hurry up and answer my prayers. Then in Christian circles, we use verses like these to remind us that God acts in His own timing and that His timing and ours are not the same. So, we are told to be patient and wait upon the Lord.

Is this what this verse means? Consider that it's just the opposite.

Could it be that the meaning of the verse is from God's perspective? God is patient with us. He knows that we take a long time to change our ways, behavior, and thoughts.

He has affirmed the fact that He has all the time in the world to wait on us as He loves us and doesn't want to lose any of us.

So, God says, "I have shown you my ways through creation, through scripture, through books, art, songs and sermons, and yet, you still struggle with trusting me." The Lord says, "I will be patient." When I look at it from His side, I'm glad He is patient for left up to me, I would have bailed long ago. From my viewpoint what I see is that the faster I can get to trust and belief, the faster I can receive God's blessing and promises.

Can I accelerate trust and belief? Can I enhance this process by what I read, attend, listen to, and watch? Hmm, something to consider?

What about the thought that we have to go through experiences to actually build trust? Does experience build trust or does trust get tested through experience?

Can we just declare now that we trust God? Can we help ourselves get there quicker by just not questioning our trust in God? After all, isn't that what happened at our point of salvation? It took me 30 years to come to faith. I hear of some who came to faith in 5 years. I guess they were quicker than me to come to the same conclusion.

I'm so glad God is patient with me.

Just a Thought…

90
More Than a Memory

As Augustine put it, "You ascended from before our eyes and we turned back grieving, only to find you in our hearts." What a beautiful quote. This we could say about most loved ones we have lost. We carry memories of these loved ones in our hearts forever.

Yet there is something significantly different with Jesus. That is the fact that Jesus is much more than a wonderful memory. He is more than someone we talk to in our quiet moments when all alone. When we pour out our hearts and souls or share our greatest victory with those embedded in our memories, we find the conversation, as sweet as it is, leaves us still alone. Yet when we engage with Jesus, we receive something back from Him. For our conversations are interactions with a living God. We can expect to receive tangible results. Not just peace of mind or comfort. We can experience real life transformation, physical and behavioral change, material blessings and true companionship.

Real things happen as if Jesus was physically standing with us wherever we are. There is no unanswered prayer. All prayers are answered according to God's timing and desired results which is always in our best interest and His. The profoundness of this is overwhelming and almost unexplainable to those who are not believers. We never need to search or call ahead or schedule an appointment. God is always with us. For it is not God who doesn't show up. Rather it is us who forget to experience His presence. In our busyness, we get caught up in ourselves and ignore our friend sitting next to us.

Yet when a need arises, we think "I can't wait to get home or go to church or go to our favorite place to meet up with Jesus." So, we drive home with great anticipation all along, missing the fact that He never left our side. Jesus is not a destination. He is the journey. Heaven is the destination. Jesus is the driver to take us there.

Just a Thought…

Love the Lord with All Your Soul

Deuteronomy 6:5
⁵ Love the Lord your God with all your heart and with all your soul and with all your strength.

God did not say, "Love the Lord with all of your time, your energy, and your resources." This is what the world says, "God wants your heart, your soul, your strength."

What's the difference? It's the cart before the horse theory.

Let's start with the heart. Why the heart? Because it is where the core desires lie and are formed. It's where the trajectory of your thoughts, actions, and deeds originate. It's where God planted Himself when He says, "I am in you."

The heart knows the person's deepest needs – the ones that get buried under the thoughts their minds conjure up. The needs of the heart are never gone, they are just forgotten and need to be awakened. The heart is what aligns itself with God. Besides its natural functions, like pumping blood through to the rest of the body, the heart is where love resides. Love needs to be received and shared; it's the fuel that keeps the organ pumping. As love begins to fade away, the pump eventually stops running and the body dies.

God knew that by asking us to love Him whole-heartedly, it would force us to fight through all the cobwebs of negative thoughts that have latched themselves on our hearts. These webs create a thick barrier that smothers it, not letting the person feel love or give it in return. God knew that the only thing that cures the heart is to love again.

By asking us to love Him whole-heartedly, our hearts would have to be healed first, refueled and ready to share again. Love ignites the ultimate weapon to flourish and experience pure joy in this world we live in. This creates a chain reaction and the world starts to come together, bringing a piece of heaven to earth.

Then there's the soul. The soul manifests the condition of one's heart. It shows us a glimpse of its state. Ask someone, "How is your soul?" and the answer will give you a looking glass into the condition of their heart. A broken heart doesn't mean a broken soul though — the souls serve as a conduit to the mind and the physical body.

The soul is where God says the spiritual battle is played out, where it uses its three weapons: the heart, the mind, and the person's strength to fend off evil. They all direct and react to determine the outcome of the battle.

Strength. This is the consolidation of the body's shell and inner parts. It's the physical expression of the condition of the heart together with the soul.

Strength is the ultimate extension of the manifestation of God. A smile generated by a pure heart and peaceful soul can render the most fortified city helpless. Using our hands and feet, we can penetrate the thickest walls of our fellow men's being.

The theory of compound interest is an example of the power of the body in alignment with the soul, which is fed by the heart. The more you deposit love, the more it compounds itself, multiplying exponentially.

A world can be changed when all three — heart, soul, and strength — are aligned. Time, energy, and resources will automatically follow as an expression of our unity with God.

Colossians 3:23-24
[23] Whatever you do, work at it with all your heart, as working for the Lord, not for human masters, [24] since you know that you will receive an inheritance from the Lord as a reward. It is the Lord Christ you are serving.

Just a Thought...

Storms

Luke 8:22-25
Jesus Calms the Storm
[22] One day Jesus said to his disciples, "Let us go over to the other side of the lake." So they got into a boat and set out. [23] As they sailed, he fell asleep. A squall came down on the lake, so that the boat was being swamped, and they were in great danger.
[24] The disciples went and woke him, saying, "Master, Master, we're going to drown!"
He got up and rebuked the wind and the raging waters; the storm subsided, and all was calm. [25] "Where is your faith?" he asked his disciples.
In fear and amazement, they asked one another, "Who is this? He commands even the winds and the water, and they obey him."

Jesus asked, "Where is your faith?" How would this story be different if the disciples had indeed shown faith?

The storm came, the winds blowing, waves crashing upon the boat and imminent danger a reality. Would the conversation go something like this? Peter would say, "Hey guys, don't worry about the storm. Hang on tight. It will get rough for a while. Maybe it will challenge us beyond our strength and even possible death, but remember Jesus is with us. Look – He is sleeping not even bothered by the storm and blatantly not concerned about death! We can be at peace for the Lord is with us! (in this case literally)

Let us consider the wonderful life we have and be at joy and peace. We don't know how or when the storm will end, but we do know it does end eventually. What remains afterward, we don't know. But what we do know is that God never left us and if we are still alive, He will help us rebuild. If we have died, we will be with our Father in heaven.

Just a side note. Did Jesus need to be woken up? Were the disciples being caring in the midst of their selfishness by waking him? Did Jesus know the storm was there even though He was asleep? Was Jesus being calm in the midst of the storm or was He a really deep sleeper? Would Jesus be mad if they didn't wake Him, so He could do his miracle? Would it be considered FAITH if the disciples woke Jesus with confidence saying, "Jesus, wake up. There is a storm and we thought you might want to do your thing, you know, calm the seas? If you don't that's okay, we just wanted to let you know is all."

What is our role in a storm? In their case, they were taking on water. Are we to do our best to fight off the storm by getting buckets and bailing water or tying down the goods or seeking shelter? If we have faith, do we just sit there a wait on God to do something?

What can we learn from this passage?

1) We know that storms come and go. Now we know they even come when God is with us in the boat.
2) We know that God rode the storm out with us.
3) We know that God could calm the storm if He saw fit to do so.
4) We know that we are not to worry about the storm.
5) We know it's okay to help defend against the storm the best we can and that starts by turning to God first. The disciples did get this right as they saw the storm and ran to Jesus.
6) We know storms will end. We will rebuild and tell stories of how we persevered. We will be a bit more confident by what we learned when the next storm comes our way.

I believe that when the disciples went on their next sailing excursion with Jesus, should a storm arise, they might have had a different perspective.

Just a Thought…

God's Economy

Consider a world where everyone follows the ways of Jesus Christ.
Now picture its effect on the business economy.
No divorce means no need for divorce lawyers.
No drugs, murder, prostitution, gambling, bars, liquor stores or porn means no police, courts, jails or prisons.
No hunger; each person will take care of the other.
No contracts; there would be no disputes.
Therapists would not be needed.
Medical treatment would be reduced by half — no addictions, starvation or assaults to treat.
No credit cards or debt management would be needed.
No security either, since no theft exist.
No gambling, no casinos.
No hatred, no betrayal, no gouging.

Satan has a major financial enterprise at stake, so he will fight aggressively.

Acts 19:23-29
The Riot in Ephesus
[23] About that time there arose a great disturbance about the Way. [24] A silversmith named Demetrius, who made silver shrines of Artemis, brought in a lot of business for the craftsmen there. [25] He called them together, along with the workers in related trades, and said: "You know, my friends, that we receive a good income from this business. [26] And you see and hear how this fellow Paul has convinced and led astray large numbers of people here in Ephesus and in practically the whole province of Asia. He says that gods made by human hands are no gods at all. [27] There is danger not only that our trade will lose its good name, but also that the temple of the great goddess Artemis will be discredited; and the goddess herself, who is worshiped throughout the province of Asia and the world, will be robbed of her divine majesty."
[28] When they heard this, they were furious and began shouting: "Great is Artemis of the Ephesians!" [29] Soon the whole city was in an uproar.

The people seized Gaius and Aristarchus, Paul's traveling companions from Macedonia, and all of them rushed into the theater together.

So, the battle rages on. Satan fights to keep his business, and God fights for His. Yet Satan refuses to acknowledge he will ultimately lose. He fights with deception, greed, power, lust, and selfishness, but God fights with truth, love, peace, patience, and kindness.

Galatians 5:19-25
[19] The acts of the flesh are obvious: sexual immorality, impurity and debauchery; [20] idolatry and witchcraft; hatred, discord, jealousy, fits of rage, selfish ambition, dissensions, factions [21] and envy; drunkenness, orgies, and the like. I warn you, as I did before, that those who live like this will not inherit the kingdom of God.
[22] But the fruit of the Spirit is love, joy, peace, forbearance, kindness, goodness, faithfulness, [23] gentleness and self-control. Against such things there is no law. [24] Those who belong to Christ Jesus have crucified the flesh with its passions and desires. [25] Since we live by the Spirit, let us keep in step with the Spirit.

We are all soldiers, and the question remains: Whose team will you be on?

Just a Thought…

94
Define Faith

Ephesians 2:8-9
⁸ For it is by grace you have been saved, through faith—and this is not from yourselves, it is the gift of God— ⁹ not by works, so that no one can boast.

Hebrew 11-1
11 Now faith is the assurance of things hoped for, the conviction of things not seen

How do we practice faith on a daily basis? How do we function by just being alive?

What happens in and around us that we can't control or have anything to do with us?

Our body functions without our control. Our mind works. Our heart beats and lungs take in breaths of air. No faith found here.

Creation exists without our control. The sun rises and sets. The stars appear and fade away. The wind blows where it pleases. Grass grows, trees blossom. animals, insects, birds of the air and fish of the sea exist without our help. No faith found here.

People are born and die, love and hate, serve and steal, encourage and oppress, without my saying so. No faith found here.

So where does faith show up, for faith is an action of intentional hope and certainty? If I eliminate the things, I have no control over, then what is left that I can apply faith to? Is faith about controlling our emotion or our belief system? Does faith, by trial and error, get replaced by fact?

Example:
I'm told that if I exercise, I will feel better and have more energy. The statement, upon first hearing, is just a thought. To take my first step requires faith. However, every day that goes by and I

exercise and experience positive results eventually, it can be medically logged and become an exact science. So now it is a fact?

The next person who is told that if they exercise, they will receive positive results are handed a factual study supporting their findings. Yet for that person to actually act on that information still requires faith. Is it faith or ignorance to take the first step? Remember, the results have been factually proven. So, what am I trusting? Could I be just being stubborn? Is it a matter of belief? It's a matter of the will?

So again, where is faith found?

Faith in God is our best example, yet even here we have enough documentation of God being real that factually supports a living God. The root of faith, I believe, shows up at the point where we reach the end of ourselves and determine that regardless of all the facts, we can't believe something is really true.

If I go to the edge of a cliff and jump, am I exercising faith? After all, it says being sure of what I hope for and certain what I can't see. When I jump, I want to be certain I won't die and sure that I will be rescued somehow.
Can faith be tested? I guess if I jump and die, my theory on faith didn't work! So, does faith have to be based upon truth? If enough people jumped before me and were rescued, does this become fact and my faith will be shored up if I try jumping myself again? What then was my faith based on? How many had to jump before me to convince me it was safe? What did the first person to jump base their faith on?

Possibly faith is a journey from the unknown to the known, from the first step of uncertainty to the next step of confidence.

Just a Thought…

95
Be Careful What You Wish For

John 15:7
⁷ If you remain in me and my words remain in you, ask whatever you wish, and it will be done for you.

"Ask whatever I wish."

God gave this same choice to Solomon and he chose wisdom. We read in Ecclesiastes that everything else Solomon tried — things we may want or have wished for — turned out to be meaningless.

Ecclesiastes 12:8
⁸ "Meaningless! Meaningless!" says the Teacher.
  "Everything is meaningless!"

Ecclesiastes 12:13-14
¹³ Now all has been heard;
  here is the conclusion of the matter:
Fear God and keep his commandments,
  for this is the duty of all mankind.
¹⁴ For God will bring every deed into judgment,
  including every hidden thing,
  whether it is good or evil.
So, what do we wish for?

We so much want to wish for the things Solomon had: money, power, pleasure, folly, wisdom, and toys. Can you feel the excitement welling up inside as you envision yourself with these things? A new car, the freedom of money and the luxury it brings, the ability to exercise power here and there, not having to strive for anything.

We want to think Solomon got it wrong. (He is a bummer to bring to your party.)

"Fear God and obey His commands." What type of gift is that to want? How will I benefit from this?

First, let's look at the gift of fearing God. What does that look like?

Fearing God is to acknowledge His supreme being, His majesty, His power, His being Lord and creator of all. His ability to be anything, to do and create anything. His rule over all that is made in the universe. His ability to know all.

When you see God for who He is, you can't help but humble yourself in a healthy, honoring fear of His presence. It's an awestruck fear.

You start seeing that all of life here on earth is tied to Him that all the things you wish for come from Him. You ask yourself, If Solomon comes to the conclusion that all we desire is meaningless, then what is left that could ever have meaning?

You experience fear then, as you sense the emptiness, the loneliness and despair. You can choose to say, "Well, Solomon may be right but who cares? I'm going for it and I will make my decision if all the things I want are meaningless, anyway." Most of us go down this path.

Yet how many times do we read stories of people who accumulated many of the things Solomon had, but hear them wish they had spent more time with their loved ones? They had found that their wealth and power and folly brought them to an unsatisfying end. If God is the only answer, then you fear losing that as well.

The second part is to obey God's commands. What are His commands? We have the Ten Commandments that tells us to put God first and honor other people. We have Jesus saying the most important command is to love your neighbor as yourself. We see it said that without love, everything else we do or say means nothing.

He asks us to seek Him and His Kingdom first, then all these things (like Solomon's things) will be given to us. The catch is that, when we seek His Kingdom first, the want and purpose for all these things, will change.

Wealth still abounds, and so do pleasure, power, passion, wisdom, and toys. But they all now have a different meaning, measurement, and purpose attached to them.

They are now used to glorify God — not pacify us.

When this change of heart happens, we can never use up all the blessings God will give us.

Obeying God's commands and fearing God is not a punishment — it's an opportunity to break the barrier of futility and experience the fullness behind a meaningful life.

Just a Thought…

96
Great Expectations

The world says, "After all, what do you expect from me?"

I expect:
That you will write the book that will teach me not to eat and how to take care of my body.
That you will provide me a job to my liking.
That you make the weather to my liking and my timing.
That I will be treated nicely and respected wherever I go regardless of my actions.
That I will always be right.
That you will always forgive me for my wrong doings.
That you will paint the next picture, write the next book, make the next movie, sing the next song, invent the next gadget, all that I may be entertained.
That I will be void of any struggles.
That you should sacrifice your life to protect me.
That you will educate me when I'm ready to learn.
That you will think about me first before yourself.
That all my physical and emotional needs will be met.
That I will be the most important above all else.

I am full of expectations of what the world is obligated to give me without me doing anything. All I can say is it's a good thing the world doesn't expect anything from me.

Just a Thought…

Faith the Size of a Mustard Seed

God says, "Faith as small as a mustard seed can move mountains." But what is this faith? What does it look like? Feel like?

As I pray, I lay my requests out before God:
Lord, heal someone. Fix this. Restore that. Bless him or her or me. Comfort us. Give us peace, rest, joy, and contentment. I need this or remove that. Change them or change the circumstances. Forgive me or them. Why or why not?

Related to faith: Is it in the answers to these prayers where mountains get moved? Or is it in the ability to let go of these prayers through the confidence in the God we submit them to?

God knows and cares enough to deal with these prayers in a way that manifests His loving character. His very desire from day one has been to love us, provide for us, and for us to love one another. In this spirit, any answer, every answer or no at answer at all to our prayers is the right answer, for God is always good.

As soon as I let go and trust Him, the mountain begins to move.

Who knows? Maybe the mountain never moved because I was holding back all this time. Just let go!

Psalms 5:3:
[3] In the morning, Lord, you hear my voice;
in the morning I lay my requests before you
and wait expectantly.

Just a Thought…

98
What Do You See?

Matthew 14:25
25 Shortly before dawn Jesus went out to them, walking on the lake.

We know the story of Jesus walking on water and how Peter got out of the boat and tried to walk on water as well. We know how that story ends. Much is written about Peter and his faith to get out of the boat, the remaining disciples who stayed in the boat, and even about Jesus on how he dealt with Peter while trying to walk on water.

I feel, at times, we get lost in the story and miss the miracle. True, the story has much meaning and application for our lives. Yes, we need the faith to get out of the boat. Yes, we need to feel encouraged that even though Peter failed to continue to walk on water, at least he got out of the boat, whereas the others never even tried. Yes, we need to see how Jesus tells us to keep our eyes on Him rather than our circumstances. All this and more are important themes of the story. Let us not overlook the real miracle of Jesus WALKING ON WATER!!

I think we tend to forget the real miracle of God each time we reduce Him to our human level and bring our circumstances into our faith. We draw the attention away from God and toward ourselves. We see that the story quickly went towards Peter and away from Jesus' miraculous ability to be walking on water and what that means.

What does Jesus walking on water mean? Do we yawn and say, "Oh well, just another cool thing God can do?" Every miracle is to be a reminder of who God is. God cannot be made small to fit our limited thinking. His miracles won't allow for that. They cause us to see beyond what this world has for us and to know that God is bigger. If we think about the miracle and what really is going on, parting of seas, bread from heaven, water from rocks, fire from heaven, rising from the grave and walking on water, we have to stop long enough to be in awe of the God we serve.

"Today, as you go about your day, look at creation and count the miracles. Then take note of how your faith grows and your worries of the day shrink away. What He desires for me is that I see "Him walking on the sea" with no shore, no success, nor goal in sight, but simply having the absolute certainty that everything is all right because I see "Him walking on the sea". – Oswald Chambers, My Utmost for His Highest

Just a Thought…

99
Can You See God?

People say they have never seen God.

I agree that no one has seen the face of God, yet I can say through faith, you will be able to see Him very clearly. When I think of people, I generally don't picture them, but rather describe them by their character or their works.

So how do I see God?

I see His creativity when I gaze upon a sunset or sunrise. I see Him when I ask, "Where did the color blue come from?" I see Him when I notice the many shades of green there are when I drive through the countryside. What was He thinking when He made a butterfly or an octopus? I see God's power when it rains, when it snows, when the waves crash along the shoreline. I see God's might when the wind blows, the stars sparkle, when the clouds cover the earth. I see Him in fire, in the sun, in the moon, and as day falls into night. I see Him as grass grows and leaves change color — all of these happens without me having anything to do with it.

I see God's passion as I peer into the innocent and wondering eyes of my grandson, who trusts all and is full of joy.

I see God's pain and tears as I watch people get hurt or abandon each other. I see His pain in the poor who are still hungry, and in single moms making it through the day. I see His pain when I visit a nursing home and see all the lonely faces of forgotten people, or when I hear about wars, torture, kidnapping, and murder.

I can see why God loves us, because this is still how He sees us. I see God's love as I watch people transform through grace as they experience His forgiveness and accept Jesus as their savior. I see is love when hope returns, when hearts are mended, and when life is restored.

I see His wisdom as I read His word through great writers who He has inspired. God's very words touch, guide, and comfort the deepest part of my soul.

I see God's joy as I watch a painting develop or as a dance take stage or as I listen to music that serenade and bring us to new places.

Because of all these, I can describe God very clearly to you. And each day I draw near Him, I see Him more clearly.

How tall is He? What color eyes or hair does He have? What color is His skin, is He stout or skinny? I don't know, and truth be told, I don't care.

I see God more clearly than I see most people directly in front of me.

Can you see Him today?

Just a Thought…

100
The Battle Begins

1Kings 11:1-4
Solomon's Wives
11 King Solomon, however, loved many foreign women besides Pharaoh's daughter—Moabites, Ammonites, Edomites, Sidonians and Hittites. ² They were from nations about which the Lord had told the Israelites, "You must not intermarry with them, because they will surely turn your hearts after their gods." Nevertheless, Solomon held fast to them in love.³ He had seven hundred wives of royal birth and three hundred concubines, and his wives led him astray. ⁴ As Solomon grew old, his wives turned his heart after other gods, and his heart was not fully devoted to the Lord his God, as the heart of David his father had been.

How, you may ask, did the wisest man in all history lose his way? I think it lies in understanding the difference between wisdom and self-will. We find that knowledge can serve us well in most areas of our life. It provides us with understanding, helps us solve complex problems, guides us in showing the right paths to take. Wisdom serves us well in teaching of others and revealing truths in our life. Yet, with all the wisdom that Solomon was given, which the bible says was the most any man ever received, it was not enough to win the battle against its greatest foe, the self-will.

We see in the story that self-will crept in slowly by Solomon marrying into other cultures. God specifically warned him to stay away from doing this. At that moment, self-will won the first of many battles to come. Solomon, I'm sure, told himself that he had enough wisdom to control that battle. However, what he didn't count on was the subtle ways that the self-will begins to erode, even our wisdom.

Over time, Solomon allowed and even supported the worship of false idols by his many wives. More and more of Solomon's will was being attacked. There comes a point where our lies begin to look like truth.

Romans 1:25
25 They exchanged the truth about God for a lie and worshiped and served created things rather than the Creator—who is forever praised. Amen.

Eventually, we are told that Solomon, the wisest, wealthiest and most powerful man in all the world came to ruin. Self-will won over wisdom in the end. Where does that leave us?

I find it interesting that Solomon asked for wisdom and yet in the end, it might have served him better to have asked for a strong self-will.

God did a wonderful thing by leveling the playing field whereas each of us, wise or not, have the same access to the only weapon that can overcome the self-will. That is God, Himself. He gave us His power through faith in His Son Jesus. After we have exhausted all our efforts and wisdom, we can ask for God's help and He will make us victorious. A word to the wise – the sooner we ask for God's help the better!

Just a Thought…

About the Author

Rich LeBrun CFB, CCIM

Rich lives in the Chicago area and is a family man. He has been married to his high school sweetheart, Cathy, for 43 years and other than his relationship with God, she has been his lifelong soul mate. He has three children and five grandchildren.

Furthermore, Rich has been blessed with many long-term friends who have walked along side of him in his spiritual journey and have generously shared their wisdom.

Rich came to know Jesus as his savior in 1985, which from that point forward, he has desired to devote the rest of his life to building this wonderful relationship.

It was about ten years ago that Rich began taking notes as to what he felt he was hearing God tell him regarding all matters of life.

About five years ago he began collecting these thoughts in his journal as a way of reminding himself of how faithful God has been in his life.

As Rich would read scripture or Christian and non-Christian books or listen to sermons or worship songs, God would impress upon him a thought and insight as to how these words or lyrics apply to everyday life. He would try to capture these impressions and share them with friends and family.

Although there were a multitude of books, sermons and songs that influenced his writings. There are a few books and authors, beyond the Bible, that inspired many of these writings which he favored and is forever grateful to those authors.

They are:

Oswald Chambers "My Utmost for His Highest"

Francois Fenelon "Let Go"

Sarah Young "Jesus Calling"

Emmet Fox "The Sermon On The Mount"

Brother Lawrence "Practicing The Presence of God"

Rich is not a pastor nor trained in theology and does not claim to understand the depth or history of Christianity, yet he does believe all followers of Jesus Christ can be inspired and spoken to just as much as the people in the Bible or writers of today, should they take the time to be alone with God, sit quietly and listen.

It is Rich's desire to share these intimate thoughts between him and God with the hope that maybe one or more may have an impact on the reader in a way that they would draw nearer to God.

Enjoy! Just a Thought!!!